Where Communism Works

Where Communism Works.

THE SUCCESS OF COMPETITIVE-COMMUNISM IN JAPAN

Douglas Moore Kenrick

President, Douglas Kenrick (Far East) Ltd.
Senior Vice-President, Asiatic Society of Japan

Charles E. Tuttle Company
RUTLAND, VERMONT & TOKYO, JAPAN

Published by the Charles E. Tuttle Co., Inc.
of Rutland, Vermont & Tokyo, Japan
with editorial offices at
2-6 Suido 1-chome, Bunkyo-ku, Tokyo 112
First published by Macmillan under the title
The Success of Competitive-Communism in Japan

© 1988 by Douglas Moore Kenrick

LCC Card No. 90-71031
ISBN 0-8048-1671-9

First Tuttle edition, 1990

Printed in Japan

Contents

Preface

Catchwords like 'Japan As Number One', 'workaholics', 'economic animals', 'rabbit hutches', 'Japan Incorporated' and 'groupism' have been coined to emphasise outstanding features of Japan. They give partial and sometimes misleading impressions. For example, 'vertical structure' and 'lifetime employment' accentuate aspects of Japan's economic system which are not unique to Japan. To understand Japanese behaviour we must delve behind the catchwords, but single-phrase descriptions, including the title of this book, usually contain grains of truth and some terms fit better than others as equipment with which to scale the high communication barriers between Japan and the outside world. 'Competitive-communism' is one.

We all harbour some impressions of Japan. Many Westerners link her with prisoner-of-war camps during the Second World War or, in recent decades, with industrial efficiency. To visualise a culture very different from our own these facts of Japan's past and present should be mixed with many others. Generalisations about nations are dangerous. There are too many exceptions. Not all individuals act in the same way. Most Japanese have been reared to live with mutual dependence and most Westeners have been taught to have faith in freedom of choice. However, I know many Japanese who are individualistic and, on the other hand, Westerners whose dependent behaviour resembles that of Japanese. Nevertheless, if they help to reduce misunderstandings, generalisations are justified.

Concrete buildings and the fashionable Western clothes of those who walk the crowded streets give an overwhelming impression that Tokyo is very similar to London, New York, Paris or any other modern twentieth-century city. And so it is. Western influence, apparent on all sides, is impossible to overlook, but even the here-today-gone-tomorrow tourists may notice outcroppings they find strange – the bowing, the shrines and temples, the festivals, the goods in some shops, the treatment they encounter – sometimes very satisfying, at other times very frustrating. Tokyo, with a population of about twelve million, has barely thirty named streets.

Similarities should not blind us to important differences. Much that is now familiar to Westerners has been adopted in little more than a hundred years. Japan has grafted industry and many Western ideas and practices on to her agricultural and 'semi-feudal' social systems while avoiding the generations of class conflict through which the West has struggled. She has been able to pick and choose while retaining many of her traditional concepts and procedures just as, after the Second World War, she selected and imported the latest machinery and techniques to rehabilitate her destroyed factories.

The Japanese work together closely in exclusive cliques which erect barricades between insiders and those outside. I hope that, when the barriers are seen, it will be possible to lower or avoid them. My Japanese friends have encouraged me not to hide the cleavages between our cultures and to write from the Western viewpoint so that they can see their country through Western eyes.

The pronouncements of people with long experience in any field should be viewed with the same caution as the assertions of those who volunteer their opinions without knowledge to back them. However, one must seek guidance if one wants an idea of what to expect of the citizens of another country. Over a decade ago, after twenty-five years of living and working and being confused in Japan, I set out to explore what lay behind Japanese behaviour that did not match with my experiences in other countries. In this presentation I give my personal view of the whole complicated and contradictory picture of Japanese behaviour and Japan's economic and social structure. I have not followed the scholarly practice of quoting a number of authorities and summing up with a guarded conclusion on each of the many limited subjects. To do so would make for a very lengthy exposition. Instead, I give my condensed conclusions interspersed with a few illustrations from relevant scholarly opinions, news items from the daily press and personal experiences. If some of my conclusions are controversial, they have been backed by much study before being summarised in their present form. The theme and title, 'Competitive-communism', has only recently emerged as the binding thread that I think accounts for Japanese success in international trade. Despite the contradictions a pattern can be discerned. It allows scope for keen competition constrained by a desire for harmony and underlying communal controls. Hyphenating 'communism' with its antithesis 'competition' highlights the contradictions and the misunderstandings that exist.

Competition (the profit motive) has been mixed into a cliquish social structure by giving pride of place to communal, person-to-person, human relations that leave limited room for aggressive individualism. The cliques raise barriers against outsiders and, to enjoy the benefits of membership, the insiders exercise constant self-control. They have security. The price is constant dependence on the communal will. The means of production have not been nationalised, but their control is in the hands of the industries themselves managed by men promoted from within their own ranks.

This book is divided into four parts. The first is an introduction to Japan's competitive-communism and a glance at the similarities and uniqueness of her culture. The second is an examination of cliques, outsiders, dependence and rationality. The third deals with the continuity and transmission of Japan's ancient social structure and the fourth gives more impressions of Japan's economic system.

The bibliography could be extended tenfold, or omitted completely. The books mentioned are a rather random selection. The various points they make may add to a beginner's confusion but may, by this, underline the difficulty of getting to grips with the contradictions that characterise Japanese behaviour.

DOUGLAS MOORE KENRICK

Acknowledgements

Permission has been granted to quote from: *The Anatomy of Dependence*, by Takeo Doi, published by Kodansha International, Tokyo, 1973; *Labour Relations in Japan Today*, by Tadashi Hanami, published by Kodansha International, Tokyo, 1979; *Never Take Yes for an Answer*, by Masaaki Imai, published by Simul Press, Tokyo, 1975; *Sixteen Ways to Avoid Saying No*, by Masaaki Imai, published by Nihon Keizai Shinbun, Tokyo, 1981; *The Japanese Language in Contempory Japan*, by Roy Andrew Miller, published by American Enterprise Institute for Public Policy Research, Washington, 1977; *The Japanese Mind*, edited by Charles A. Moore, published by Charles E. Tuttle Company, Tokyo, 1973.

The British Ambassador to Japan, Sir John Whitehead, has permitted the inclusion of his masterful summary of developments in Japan over the last thirty years and his thoughts on Japan's future as expressed in his address to an international symposium held by the *Japan Times* to celebrate its ninetieth anniversary in 1987.

My helpful and conscientious secretary Yoko Nishikata, without whose hours of typing this book could not have reached its present form, has earned a whole-hearted tribute. From a chaos of lengthy extracts from the works of dozens of scholars whose research has given foundation to many of my dogmatic assertions, she has typed and retyped a multitude of words as I assembled and reassembled my thoughts. I believe Yoko-san has had her own satisfaction in doing a demanding job willingly. She has immeasurably eased my burden as taskmaster and has given ample evidence of the best side of the Japanese work ethic.

D.M.K.

Part I
Introduction

1 Competitive-Communism

JAPANESE PRACTICE, COMMUNIST THEORY

Any abbreviation is inadequate as a comprehensive description of a country's social structure but 'competitive-communism' serves as a measuring stick and as a realistic vantage point from which to view the working of Japanese society. The word 'communism' has many very different meanings. This book is mainly concerned with one standard dictionary definition, 'communal living, communalism', but it cannot overlook the usual, 'advocacy of a classless society in which private ownership has been abolished and the means of production and subsistence belong to the community'. This book is not political and does not set out to explore the ways that the ideas set out by Marx have been interpreted by theoreticians and practised by the governments of communist countries. To avoid emotional repercussions generated by mention of the word communism, perhaps 'communalism' could be substituted or a new word 'competunism' coined to incorporate the contradictory element of competition. However, the combination 'competitive-communism' seems a more appropriate label. It emphasises that Japan has developed an advanced, bureaucratic, economic and social system that is different from, as well as similar to, 'capitalism'. The 'communism' of 'competitive-communism' is spelled with a small 'c'.

Of course, Japan is not dominated politically by 'a movement or a political party advocating and affirming the need for a dictatorship of the proletariat'. Such a movement based on Western concepts does not fit the Japanese post-war scene. Far from it. The great majority of the Japanese people react against state dictatorship and certainly do not think of themselves as communists or as members of the proletariat. Coupling 'competitiveness' with 'communism' implies the opposite of rigid, centralised, state-control usually associated with the governments of present-day Communist states. The making of profit is at the core of Japan's economy.

Although it is communalism that comes closer to the way the Japanese work together let us first look briefly at the similarities and differences between Japanese practice and some interpretations of Marxian theories. The main aims attributed to Soviet Communism

3

are the public ownership of property, a classless society and a dictatorship by the workers until these aims have been achieved. Each element is reflected in Japan and, for that matter, to a much lesser degree, may also be found in Western capitalistic democracies. A comparison between Japanese practice and these extreme communist aims shows some resemblances but little close correspondence.

PUBLIC OWNERSHIP OF PROPERTY

Most property in Japan is now privately owned. However, until a century and less ago, most was held in common by 'extended-families' which can also be called 'extended-households'. (They were quite different from the large Indian and Chinese families which 'extend' to include all blood relatives living in other households. Children, or adults, who left the Japanese 'extended-family' completely lost membership and their rights to all but personal possessions.)

The Japanese have always been clear-headed and materialistic in their priorities – people live on the income they generate. In rice-farming communities, co-operation was necessary for the growing, harvesting and sale or exchange of the crop. Each household, organised to farm collectively, exercised social discipline through its own systematised hierarchy. Help during planting and harvesting, and loans of farm implements or money, were given between main and branch extended families which also combined in village communities to share common interests in forests and mountains, the irrigation of paddy-fields, religious ceremonies, fire control, road mending, canal-clearing and excommunication of those who offended social norms. Property was held collectively by the extended household.

The effects of urbanisation and working in companies must not be underestimated, of course, but in the cities and factories the old spirit of mutual expectations and dependency persist. The fundamental fraternal belongingness and exclusivity, and the communal dependence of its members who have not sought to be self-contained individuals, have remained unchanged. The values that characterise ancient societies have been retained, adjusted and refined to meet the needs of the modern community with the contemporary modification that the extended-household has become the place-of-work fraternity and property is held by individuals rather than collectively.

The earlier communal ownership of property has not given place to public ownership by the government. Nowadays land and house ownership is similar to that in 'capitalist' countries. Japanese buy their own houses, or invest in shares, restricted only by their income, not by state control. Few Japanese enterprises are nationalised. Almost all are 'owned' by shareholders, but a new form of communal organisation has been introduced. There is little effective private control of large-scale industry. The shareholders have little influence over the administration of their investments. Company directors in practice do not acknowledge that private shareholders are entitled to any say in the management. In one extreme case, in 1980, a group of speculators bought seventy per cent of the shares of the Miyaji Iron Works by purchases through the Stock Exchange. (I held shares in this company which I bought at about 160 yen and sold at an average price of about 300 yen. The speculators pushed the market price to about 700 yen.) The directors prevented them appointing new directors and taking over the management of the company. Private shareholding disguises communal control from within companies.

In Western countries the shareholders have a hand in policy making by appointing and dismissing the directors. They often choose a majority from men with experience and influence in other companies or professions, men whose main aim is to see that the company makes a profit each year and that the shareholders receive the largest feasible dividends. On paper the Japanese follow similar procedures but the process was modified at the outset a hundred years ago. Aspiring industries were initiated or financed by the government and, when established on a profitable footing, a few families and some institutions received the shares. Most directors were (and still are) appointed and replaced by promotion of fellow workers from within the company. Alongside them on the board may be a few directors representing major shareholders, or banks, or associated companies, or creditors with large financial stakes, but the other organisations, in their turn, ignore their own private shareholders.

Control of the capital invested is the prerogative of company directors. Dividends are very low. Most profits are retained for the benefit of the companies, not distributed to 'capitalist' shareholders. Fortunately for management, shares are bought for capital gain, not for significant dividends. The average yield of a share on the Tokyo Stock Exchange stands at less than two per cent on its market price which can be from ten to six hundred times its face value. A share's price can fall by 50 per cent or rise by 100 per cent in the course of any year, or any month. (At the time I wrote this paragraph shares in Iino Kaiun rose from about 150 yen to about 450 yen within a week or so and to 600 yen a little later.) The government does not discourage private investors from making capital gains.

The directors themselves, the most senior employees, have an advantage over their juniors. Legally, they are representatives of the shareholders. Promotion to director extends the benefit of 'lifetime' employment beyond the strictly enforced retirement age which varies from company to company. Until recently this was between 55 to 60 years old, but it is now being extended beyond 60. Directors of large Japanese companies are older than their Western counterparts and, with a few exceptions, are workers who have survived the weedings-out. Generally they have had to spend about 37 years with the same company to climb to the top. Having joined at about 23 years old they may become presidents at about 60. However, if small corporations are included, top management in Japan is steadily becoming younger.

Annual general meetings of shareholders follow Western procedures but, with rare exceptions, they are sparsely attended and often rush through their business in less than twenty minutes. This has been achieved partly by the directors hiring *sokaiya*, professional holders of shares, who look for failures in a company's performance or balance sheet and threaten the management. *Sokaiya* support or oppose managements depending on how much they are paid. The Commercial Law was revised in October 1982 to punish companies which paid *sokaiya*. At that time there were said to be about 6800 *sokaiya* with a total annual income of about twenty billion yen. The number was thought to have fallen to about 400 by mid-1984 when, in the first court-case under the amended law, a senior staff member of a large department store and six *sokaiya* were prosecuted, found guilty and fined for paying and receiving monies to influence the conduct of the company's annual general meeting of shareholders. The influence of *sokaiya* has been reduced, but not eliminated.

The Japanese company is not a complex of workers, managers and directors with conflicting interests. All aim to make their companies profitable and to retain the profits within 'their' companies. This communal control of industry by industry for the benefit of industry lies between 'public' and 'private' ownership. It dominates the Japanese economic structure which does not encompass much nationalisation of industry, but has diminished the reality of private ownership. This gives some justification for the label 'competitive-communism'.

CLASSLESS SOCIETY

The Japaneese live within rigid hierarchies. Each person's status is most carefully defined, but grades depend more on educational attainment, ability and personal friendships than on family background or wealth. Constant changes of grade override class distinctions of the West.

Over 80 per cent of the Japanese people in 1985 described themselves as middle class. A poll by the Prime Minister's Office in 1984 had reported that about 90 per cent identified themselves with the middle class. Of the ten thousand surveyed, all aged over twenty, 55 per cent ranked themselves as 'middle of the middle class', 27 per cent as 'lower level of the middle class', and 8 per cent as 'upper level of the middle class'. The 1985 classification divided the 'middle class' into 'upper' and 'lower' only. All these percentages depend very much on definition of who is 'middle class'.

Since the mid nineteen-seventies differences in the ownership of wealth and of wage differentials have become noticeably greater. Income differentials were small between 1955 and 1975. There are still very few super-rich, but differentials are growing. Some cynics say that the Japanese should not call themselves middle class. They explain that the Japanese are still comparing their life-styles with pre-war impoverishment and that it is a Japanese characteristic that everyone's aim is to be the same as the neighbours. It may be wish fulfilment, rather than economic reality, but a vast majority of Japanese consider themselves middle class. In doing so they are the same as many Westerners who consider themselves 'middle class' even when their incomes are lower than those of many of the 'working class'.

The early years of industrialisation from the 1870s onwards saw cheap labour readily available and a temporary break between the poverty but security of farm labour and the development of 'lifetime' industrial employment. The break was, however, fairly short-lived and the deep roots of the extended-household survived to sustain,

after the Second World War in a new form, the relations inherited
from agricultural communities. The European factory system has
been embraced in Japan without generations of bitter and sustained
class struggle which in some other countries has established impersonal battle lines between workers and capitalists. Workers and
management are not at arm's length, as in the West where companies
treat labour as expendable. Labour relations in Japan are as much
personal as contractual. A communistic feeling that the place-of-
work, the corporation, exists for the employees and to give a service
to its customers, not the shareholders, is taken for granted.

In capitalist countries most workers have little in common with
their employers. They feel that if they work harder or more carefully
it is the 'capitalists' who reap the profit from their efforts. In Japan
the workers feel that they benefit from the success of their own
company, that if it fails they lose their otherwise secure income. The
Westerner lives with the prospect that no matter how conscientiously
he has worked, or how high he has risen, he may at any time be
discharged at short notice. He does not have the feeling of security
enjoyed by his Japanese counterpart.

Irrespective of their rank within each hierarchy, the Japanese treat
one another as fellow human beings. Their communal system does
not produce the assertive self-righteous individualism and lack of
concern for others that one finds so conspicuous in Europe and
America. Since everyone relies for material rewards and ego
fulfilment on acceptance by his intimates, each gains satisfaction by
doing his or her job properly. A waitress in a society that exalts
independence may with a snarl throw the food at customers and
sometimes does so to prove her independence. In Japan a waitress
plays her part or risks being ostracised by her fraternity. She smiles
at the customer.

In June 1983 the press published two newsworthy rather than
typical examples of the tendency towards equality in Japanese
organisations:

> Hoya City in western Tokyo had, for eighteen years (since
> April 1965), been paying city officials a uniform wage based solely
> on age irrespective of the type of work with the exception that
> management-level officials (section chiefs and above) received a
> small addition (yen 62,000 per month for department chiefs and
> yen 48,000 for section chiefs). Lower rankers could earn more
> than this increment from overtime pay and therefore could receive

more at the end of the month than a manager who was not entitled to overtime pay. The system had been adopted at the insistence of the union of city employees on the grounds that family financial needs were roughly the same for all employees of the same age.

Shoichiro Toyoda, president of the Toyota Motor Company, the world's second largest automobile maker with surplus funds of about a trillion yen, was setting an example of frugal living. It was said that he had his shoes resoled until they wore out and his wife wore ready-made clothes. Vice-presidents and lower ranking Toyota board members refrained from buying new cars. The company had recently held a three-day study meeting for its forty-four executive-board members at a dormitory of a Toyota subsidiary, not at a luxury hotel. They had been asked to bring their own bath towels and to accept the same conditions as newly enrolled employees. Classes, from 8 a.m. to 11 p.m. had included lectures by university professors and group discussions about total quality control.

Some observers claim that the workers of post-war Japan have not benefited to the same degree that the wealth of the country has grown. A large segment of profits has been retained by the companies which have generated them and wage increases have to be set against the higher cost of living, but the Japanese are no longer a 'poor' people. Real incomes are about three times higher than they were thirty years ago. The security given by 'lifetime' employment is a step towards communistic ideals and graduated income tax and social security services play some part in equalising incomes. Death duties range up to higher percentages than in most other countries.

Apart from income recorded in statistics, the Japanese system incorporates a wide variety of fringe benefits. Some such as company housing and sponsored leisure activities are open. Some are concealed. Company managers, themselves 'workers', divert much expenditure for the personal betterment of the employees. Of course, the higher the status of the employee the more he receives in this way, but most gain some advantages. The National Tax Administration reports that Japanese business spends on entertainment a gigantic amount (in 1984 3620 billion yen, more than thirteen billion pounds sterling) a sum that exceeds or approaches the government's expenditure on defence or education. It is also more than the amount paid as dividends to shareholders. Since entertainment – wining and dining, golf, mah-jong and gift-giving – includes the hosts as well as the guests, and is often balanced by reciprocal entertainment, many employees raise their standard of living well beyond recorded figures.

In Japan the higher-salaried senior pays a heavy price in the social obligations he must accept. To encourage a following he must sacrifice much of his time to his subordinates. He spends two or more evenings every week meeting them in places of relaxation. He leans on his more energetic and able juniors and gives them prestige. Most effective managers act as part of their fraternities, not as individuals above them.

Thirty years ago incomes at the top were very low by any standards. Now they are substantially higher, but this conforms with communist practice if not theory. Soviet Communist countries reward their élites. In Japan it may be said that there is a definite tendency for people to work according to their ability and to be paid according to their needs. As the Japanese people think of themselves as classless, one theoretical aim of communism would appear to have already been achieved in practice.

DICTATORSHIP BY THE WORKERS

Dictatorship by the workers boils down in practice to dictatorial control by the workers' representatives. The Diet, Japan's parliament, is elected along democratic lines although the cost of standing for a seat is very high and electors do not set up grassroots organisations to finance their political choices. In Japan candidates form their own support organisations and rely for the huge funds they need on a small number of financially strong sources – their party, their friends and businesses. Rather than raising contributions from the voters, they may even pay electors to vote for them. This could lead to autocratic rule but, so far, political parties, both those in power and those in opposition, have divided themselves into competing factions, or cliques, and no single faction has emerged strong enough to exercise anything approaching dictatorship.

In the Japanese business world there is reluctance to give sole authority to a man at the top. In the West high position carries autocratic decision-making power. The president of a Japanese company also makes final decisions but, more often than not, approves, or disapproves, proposals already screened by his juniors. The Japanese depend on a consensus. With exceptions, a dictatorial head is less acceptable than one who puts reliance in his team.

A parallel to communist organisation is notable in the extensive bureaucratic structure of the Japanese economy. In spite of keen competition within the political, civil service and business corridors of power, bureaucratic practice has played a part in the adoption of the rather misleading catch-word, 'Japan Incorporated'.

At a symposium in Japan in 1983 Ronald Dore aptly pin-pointed Japan's uniqueness as an industrial power 'in its achievement in harnessing bureaucratic forms to the production of goods and services'. He pointed out that,

> In large "capitalist" industrial firms lifetime employment, career grades based on educational achievement, incremental wage scales within these grades, promotion up the hierarchy of ranked offices by a mixture of seniority and merit criteria is, of course, precisely the standard employment system of government bureaucracies in Europe; the civil service, the armed forces and the police.

To these characteristics of Japanese businesses he extends the communal hierarchy to include 'dominant firms and their client subcontractor suppliers bound by relations' and 'a network of producer "guilds" which regulate the terms of competition between competitors' together with 'a system of government supervision, partly statutory and partly by "administrative guidance".' 'These seemingly diverse features,' he concludes, 'are all of one piece. As mechanisms for motivating economic activity they rely not merely on individual pursuit of self interest but also on some sense of loyalty to the larger unit, some identification with its goals . . . , and loyalty of individual industries and their constituent firms to the nation.' (I would substitute the word 'dependence' for 'loyalty').

Bureaucracy is a tool of dictators. It opposes freedom of choice. In commerce and industry as well as the civil service, Japan has an efficient bureaucratic framework which regulates the compulsions of profitability, competition and consensus decision making.

In addition to bureaucracy, another sign-post pointing to communistic tendencies in Japan comes closer to justifying the common abbreviation, 'Japan Incorporated'. The idea that a country is 'incorporated' implies the centralised, regulated control exemplified by an incorporated company with a president and board of directors dictating and implementing policies. In a later chapter I will argue that Japan is 'unincorporated' in a Western sense although it is in fact dominated by a communistic, communal system of inter-dependence that consolidates and motivates its society.

JAPAN'S COMPETITIVE-COMMUNISM

Comparing Japan's social and economic organisation with those of today's communist countries gives a hint of competitive-communism, but the whole picture is seen only if we include as communism the communal living practised in primitive societies before the development of feudalism and then of capitalism. The amazing feature of Japan is that it has by-passed much of the underlying social organisation that has been created during the growth of today's Western industrial societies.

Japan has industrialised and learned the techniques of commerce most successfully but, in doing so, has not adopted much that we take for granted in the West. The Japanese structure is poles apart from Western capitalism and Soviet communism. It reflects a different interpretation of and an alternative to both. The whole picture has to be seen if we are to weigh the advantages against the disadvantages of borrowing from Japan.

The characteristics of ancient social organisation, in modern dress, include the cellular, cliquish organisation of Japanese society which creates high barriers between 'insiders' and 'outsiders'; a hierarchy of clearly defined grades; a practical rather than rational approach to problems; and legal practice at variance with Western norms.

Competition at all levels has profound effects but, at the root of the complex social organisation is 'dependence', in contrast to the individualism that moulds other peoples. Reliance on others is cultivated by "human relations", intimate person-to-person alliances which, in turn, demand conformity, self-control, and consensus decision-making. Mutual dependence is Japan's strength and weakness and gives an underlying unity which brings the broad picture into focus. Communal, or communistic, living together, and its effects, will be described in the chapters that follow.

Japan has made little conscious effort to achieve communism. The very weakness of political struggle for the establishment of a Soviet system could reflect conservatism and satisfaction with capitalist practices, but it could also indicate the extent to which communistic aims are already met within an economy dominated by the profit motive.

2 Beneath the Western Veneer

SIMILARITIES

Before seeking further evidence of competitive-communism and other unusual features of Japan, let us look first at characteristics and customs which are not basically different from those of other countries even though some, at first glance, appear to be dissimilar. Her fabulous industrial growth since 1945 has inspired and coloured much that is thought and written about Japan. Visitors live in standardised, Western-style hotels, they travel in speedy 'bullet-trains'. Even in the remote countryside they will see large modern factories. Only a few non-Japanese live for any time in Japanese-style inns. Even fewer visit or live in Japanese homes. They are shown, if they are willing, innumerable shrines and temples, but their greatest impression is likely to be that Japan resembles their own countries. A book could be written about similarities and might help communication between peoples, but would it overcome basic misunderstandings?

The Japanese are not strange beings, nor biologically unique, nor different in all aspects of their culture. They are not creatures from outer space. From time to time over the years I have been annoyed by some Japanese behaviour only to encounter, on my next trip outside Japan, the same things that bothered me. We inhabit vast areas in common and in the same way. The distinctive characteristics of the Japanese are the products of their culture which minimise, or exaggerate, universal human traits. That much of their behaviour is recognisable to Westerners as parts of our own make-up gives a solid basis for mutual understanding.

Asian people have a distinctive cast of countenance, skin colour-ation and hair-growth but the Japanese people physically resemble Chinese, Koreans and other Asians and, nowadays, many Europeans and Americans whose parents were Asians.

To dispose of the physical differences between Japanese and other Asians, I cite the wartime experience of my friend, a pure Japanese, Yagi-san, who worked for a Japanese trading company in Hong

Kong when the colony was occupied by Japan. On three occasions the Japanese military police threw him into jail and beat him up. They thought from his physical appearance and speech that he was a Chinese masquerading as a Japanese and perhaps spying. In 1948 Yagi-san looked Japanese to my inexperienced eye. He continued unchanged until his death in 1982. No wonder I am cynical of the judgement of many Westerners I meet who claim positively to be able to distinguish at a glance without hearing them speak between Japanese and Chinese and, by implication, Koreans, Taiwanese and other Asians.

While biological differences do not constitute uniqueness, it should be noted that research at present being undertaken by Tadanobu Tsunoda points to the possibility that the left hemisphere of the Japanese brain may respond to sounds that trigger the right hemispheres of most of the rest of the world's population. He is convinced that he has solid scientific evidence that the brain functioning of Japanese people brought up in a Japanese environment does not fit the pattern of people brought up in other environments. He does not attribute this to heredity. His findings are not yet generally accepted. If they are refuted, or confirmed as positive proof of uniqueness, hardly a word of this book will need to be changed.

Japanese culture is now camouflaged under a thick layer of Western usages. To examine what is submerged below we may be guided, or confused, by customs. It is easy to write a book filled with examples of exotic and inconsequential customs, some sensible, others not. However, what first inspires the pens of Western newcomers rarely reveals the motivations for contradictory behaviour that confuse most Westerners who stay for a long time in Japan. Things that strike one first are often the least significant.

When I first took a bath the Japanese way, the soaping and washing outside the bath before immersing disturbed my long-established habits. The water scalded me. One day a Japanese girl asked how we bathed in the West. I told her. She looked at me wide-eyed and exclaimed, 'Do you really mean that you wash in the bath and lie in the dirty water?' I learned that a hot bath can be for relaxing, not washing. With practice I became used to cleansing my body thoroughly outside the bath and, by easing into the steaming water with a minimum of splashing, the shock became bearable. In my home I now prefer the clean and refreshing Japanese bath.

Another Japanese custom which I have adopted is to take off my shoes and put on slippers when entering my house. It must be cleaner than treading in dirt from the streets. However, I do not take off my slippers when entering my rooms as I have carpeted floors. It would, of course, be obligatory in a Japanese home with its floor made of heavy grass matting that is slept on without the benefit of a Western-style bed. I prefer Western flooring and furniture.

The temperature at which food is served is often less than satisfactory to Westerners. Over the years many of my friends, when staying at Japanese-style inns, have tried to obtain their Western-style ham and eggs served hot. Language is not the barrier. I have breakfasted with a Japanese friend in one of Japan's finest old inns. He placed the order. In one extreme case friends placed their breakfast order the night before for delivery at 8 a.m. the next morning. Breakfast was served on time but the ham and eggs had been cooked the previous night, stored in the refrigerator, and were rimmed with ice when placed on their table.

These Japanese customs give ambiguous guidance unless taken at more or less than their face value. The method of bathing, for instance, reflects not just Japanese cleanliness but also an extremely practical approach to living. One bathful of water shared by every member of the family saves fuel. The large neighbourhood public bath is also economical and it brings a local community into person-to-person daily contact. Changes of footwear inside the Japanese house are simply the product of matted floors and one must be cautious not to infer too much from variations in the temperatures at which food is served. Many conservative inn-keepers have yet to appreciate the importance of temperature to some of the Westerners' diets.

These, and other manifestations of Japan's culture, like waving to signal approach rather than departure, the non-use of first names, bowing and skill in grilling eels to create a gourmet's dream, can be recounted endlessly. Such intriguing practices have little influence on decision making by management or the motivation of workers. On the other hand, it is hardly too much to say that the less obvious an action the greater its weight. For intance, a pause in conversation before a reply may be more important than the words that follow. A Japanese hesitates to cause embarrassment or to disturb harmony by directly stating harsh facts or opinions and is as concerned with what is not said as with what is said.

Many Japanese customs and habits deviate substantially from

Western norms but, though they may sometimes mislead Westerners, have no place in a serious discussion about uniqueness. For example, some think of suicide as a Japanese speciality. Ceremonial death by plunging a sword into one's belly, so at variance from the Christian ethic which prohibits self-slaughter, was condoned by law and custom in Japan's past. However, the West gives social approval to heroes and captains who go down with their ships. Though some suicides had special significance in Japan in the past and nowadays the Japanese reasons for committing suicide tend to differ from those of Westerners, international statistics show fewer suicides as a percentage of population in Japan than in eight European countries.

Many other Japanese customs reveal similarities between our cultures and meld with manifestations of Western influence. Justifiably impressed by the gigantic changes in the environment in recent decades, many Westerners believe that the Japanese have become Westernised. A founder of the world-famous Sony company once said that Japanese managerial practice is 95 per cent the same as the Western, but the other 5 per cent is, if I remember his words correctly, 1000 per cent different. Similarities are great but must be measured against deep-rooted cultural values.

MYSTERY?

Most Japanese people, including scholars, believe that their culture is mysterious and inexplicable and, despite the many recognisable features, some Westerners share this belief. Mystery is a comfortable refuge for those who prefer not to see what stares them in the eye. Charles Lamb once said he believed there were fairies at the bottom of his garden, but he would not go to look in case he could not find them. For those, including many Japanese, who wish to blinker themselves with mysticism and myth and blindly to accept inexplicable 'reason beyond reason', there can always be mystery. But there need be no such curtain to hide an understanding of the Japanese people and their social and economic system.

In sailing ship days Westerners thought of Japan as mysterious, an exotic, distant land inhabited by fierce, two-sworded warriors who wrote poetry, arranged flowers and drank tea with great ceremony. They were entertained by enchanting, peach-skinned geisha girls. Much water has flooded and dried on the paddy fields. The romantic image has faded.

The dreaded, fanatic warriors of only a generation ago, dressed in khaki uniforms and armed with effective aeroplanes and modern military equipment, have given way to a so-called self-defence force, large but rarely in evidence. Nowadays beautiful hostesses in evening gowns and the latest Western hair-styles charm in thousands of places of entertainment, but few geisha remain among them. To the surprise of some Westerners, the most popular are frequently neither young nor beautiful. There need be no surprise, of course, if we realise that geisha have achieved their importance by their skill in flattering and in helping their clients to relax. They are well-trained and highly accomplished entertainers. Beauty helps but is only one attribute and can be secondary.

Japan avoided the white man's colonial yoke and, after the last hundred years of chequered international relations, has now taken her place as a great industrialisd country, dominant in many sectors of world trade. She is close to everywhere in our jet-shrunk world. Cheap, high quality radios, television sets, computers and cars conjure up a very modern image though, to most Japanese and to some Westerners, mystery still shrouds the Land of the Rising Sun.

In the last decade scholars, Japanese and foreign, have formulated a gaggle of new interpretations of Japanese cultural values and the reasons for their existence. They have lit torches which illuminate some previously hidden features and which show in a clearer light others which had been but dimly discerned. All find extreme divergencies between Japanese culture and those of other countries. Some refute the conclusion that the differences constitute uniqueness, others assert it, but there can be differences, and even uniqueness, without mystery.

The Japanese have developed a highly successful way of living together and have embraced much that is common in the West. However, it is no exaggeration to say that aliens (to the Japanese every non-Japanese is an alien) who have learned the language and have spent more than six months in the country experience much that is contradictory. They can be quite as confused as people who have not visited Japan. There are things that set the Japanese apart and that are hard to reconcile.

The well-known contradictoriness of Japanese behaviour makes it quite possible for the same observer to write two entirely different accounts of almost every aspect of Japanese society and to substantiate each with loads of evidence. Contradictions have often been listed in abbreviations such as: tradition as opposed to modernity;

self-control v. emotionalism; dependency v. egoism; politeness v. rudeness; submission v. aggression; competition v. communism. These extravagant extremes of behaviour and custom are to be found in all countries, but the disparities are greater and more frequently displayed in Japan. The difficulty is to reconcile the extremes, but they should not give a false impression that Japan is mysterious.

Contact with Japanese teaches one to expect the unexpected. We can be stimulated if, with hindsight, we work out the reasons and emotions behind the unexpected words or deeds. Failure to fathom the background can be frustrating.

The behaviour of the Japanese is often confusing, frequently contradictory and sometimes unpredictable. As individuals they may sometimes be inscrutable and they may have some unique qualities, but they need no longer be mysterious.

UNIQUENESS

European and American nations have been in such close contact for so long that their citizens can readily recognise the differences among themselves. The Japanese have been at arms length from all other countries for many centuries. While they have assimilated much from outside they have retained some ways of life which are hard to reconcile with Western equivalents.

Every person is unique. Every language is unique. Some may say that every country's social structure is unique. This does not mean that persons, languages and social structures do not have much in common with other persons, languages and social structures. Whatever the subject of our enquiry we must accept that our subject is unique if we are to describe and compare its characteristics. To me this is self-evident and platitudinous but to say that the Japanese are unique raises much controversy.

If the Japanese are in some ways extremely different from the peoples of other nations, to call them unique effectively tells us of the need to examine the divergencies. A more diplomatic word would be 'apart' but 'unique', as a contentious term, scratches more deeply the Western veneer that conceals significant facets of Japan's traditional culture.

'Uniqueness' is such a categoric and emotive term that, when applied to a nation, it must be used with care, but unique behaviour and a unique social system are, as such, neither better nor worse than other behaviour and social systems. Few individuals and no nations are identical and sweeping differences under the carpet solves nothing. The daily lives of persons and countries hinge on knowing and coping with differences. Distinctions should be isolated, described and analysed. Ignorance clouds real issues.

Whatever terms are used, most Japanese sincerely believe that they are unique and, equally sincerely, that foreigners cannot understand them. They feel no compulsion to examine and explain their uniqueness to outsiders, or to themselves, nor have they the Westerner's urge to fathom in what ways they are unique. While conceding that not many aliens understand the Japanese, it could be argued that few Japanese understand themselves. Whatever our country, we tend to accept uncritically and without thought things to which we have been born. Gaps in our knowledge of ourselves, our habits and our customs are common to all peoples, but especially to the Japanese.

My use of the word 'unique' to describe the Japanese social structure has been challenged by some of my friends (Japanese, American, French, Dutch). A few feel that the differences are superficial, others believe that we should emphasise similarities and turn a blind eye to deviations even if they are substantial. One man has written to a local newspaper:

> There is nothing new . . . in the idea that the Japanese are completely different from the rest of the world. They want to capitalize on their differences. There are indications that some segments of Japanese society are tending again in the direction of nationalistic tendencies, that smack of pre-war militarism. We must emphasize similarities between countries if we are to live together in one small world.

The warning must be borne in mind but to acknowledge uniqueness is definitely not to encourage or approve of racialism or militarism. It is natural to have pride in oneself, one's family, home, town and country but one must also accept the pride of others. To be nationalistic does not prevent our being internationalistic now that the world is so small and events in other countries have such strong repercussions in our own. There are, however, degrees in nationalist emotions from person to person and country to country. It should never be overlooked that the majority of the Japanese are more intensely nationalistic than the majority of the people in other countries. Some commentators have gone so far as to say that nationalism is Japan's religion.

Awareness of themselves as a very distinct and cliquish nation has been fostered for the last three or four generations and has become a conspicuous Japanese characteristic. To build Japan as a strong nation capable of withstanding colonisation by a world power, its politicians and bureaucrats and, under their direction, educators indulged in a great flood of propaganda and public relations to impress their Japanese nationality on all their citizens.

Nyozekan Hasegawa writing in 1940 under government sponsorship at the height of pre-war militarism exemplifes this indoctrination and reflects the pattern of thought to which now senior Japanese were educated and which has coloured the feelings of the present generation. He wrote:

'The history of no other country in the world mirrors the past and present-day character of the nation with as much clarity and precision as that of Japan. This unique feature arises from the fact that few nations in the world have succeeded in maintaining, unbroken and almost unaltered, since prehistoric times up to the present, the essence, character, and form of the racial group in the way the Japanese have done . . . Here is a racial group which has succeeded for a period of thousands of years, within the same area and under the same line of rulers, in perpetuating without any revolutionary changes and in developing without interruption a civilization that has remained steadfastly the same in essence as in origin . . . The national ideology which prevailed in Japan tens of centuries ago is still in force today. In the matter of government Japan has gone through the period of the clan system, centralization of power, Imperial rule, regency, and the constitutional system, but the basic principles of her national law and system of jurisprudence have remained as solidly intact as those adopted at the time of the birth of the Empire twenty-six centuries ago. By the constitution enacted in the 22nd year of Meizi [sic] (1889), there were adopted such institutions as are embodied in modern constitutions in the West . . . These basic principles of national law were not founded, as in the case of European countries, on new-born political ideologies in modern States, but were no other than a presentation in modern dress of the principles which, from ancient times, had existed as the fundamentals of law or established ideologies of government . . . The constancy of the character of Japanese history is accounted for by the fact that the character of the ancient Japanese State was such as to be adaptable to a modern State.'

In 1979, Yoshizane Iwasa, adviser to the Fuji Bank and vice-president of the Federation of Economic Organisations gave a more balanced statement of the case today for opening our eyes to Japanese 'uniqueness'.

On the surface, we have adopted Western-style clothes, food and houses and other things to quite an extent and we have become rapidly and highly Westernized in many aspects. However, if you go a little deeper, the Japanese are still different. Our way of thinking, our logic is different from those of our Western counterparts. And this applies to the management of the national economy and of business enterprises where economic laws and management principles dictate one's actions. What we Japanese regard as an accepted way of doing things is not necessarily so for Westerners. As interdependent relations deepen among countries, these differences become more apparent and more serious. What different peoples accept as common practice among themselves become more conspicuous, and there lies the source of difficulty in international relations and mutual understanding . . . We must realize that there are differences, understand them and accept them.

A current example of nationalism is the Education Ministry's instructions to the publishers of school text books to use euphemisms in describing Japan's militaristic expansion before and during the Pacific War. The policy had been enforced from 1957, but became an international controversy in 1982 when China, Korea and other countries protested vigorously against the virtual banning of such words as *shinryaku* (aggression or invasion) and *Nippon no teikoku-shugi* (Japanese imperialism) from history text-books. The Pacific War had to be called the Great East Asia War. Although this has been an instance of extreme nationalism by the government, the general public, or at least Japanese newspapers and other media, have taken a strong stand against it.

Japan is not the same as the West in many ways. A major American toy manufacturer with a market in eighty-seven countries publishes an elaborate product catalogue which he uses in every country but one. He recognizes the needs of the Japanese market. He redesigns many of his toys in colour, shape and physical appearance and publishes a separate catalogue for Japan.

Let us remember that, whatever non-Japanese say or think, the Japanese themselves have a deep belief that they are different from all other people. By awareness we may help to diminish the extreme of nationalism, but let us not be diverted by subjective arguments about similarities, mystery and uniqueness. The way the Japanese people live and work together is shown quite objectively in the way they organise themselves into cliques which generate dependence and which effectively dominate the country.

Part II

Communistic Behaviour and Social Structure

3 Cliques

The Japanese submerge themselves in exclusive cliques bound together in rigid hierarchies and protected by high barriers from all who are outsiders. The word 'group' has been and is widely used to describe the clusters into which the Japanese social system is fragmented, but group does not convey with sufficient strength the tight manner in which the Japanese band together for mutual dependence and belongingness. 'Families' would be an excellent substitute, but the idea of families without blood-ties is so divorced from Western concepts that it could create misunderstanding.

'Clique' more accurately defines the exclusivity of a Japanese group which works together and contends in contradictory ways. Cliques are 'bodies of people whose members, united in aims and interests, work with one another for common goals which take priority over each individual's and all outsiders' interests'. Individuals are so moulded by their cliques that their behaviour is comprehensible only when related to communal pressures. Although there are many exceptions, it is safe to generalise that conformity is the rule in Japan.

Cliquish organisation is common in all bureaucratic establishments and equally standard in large Japanese commercial and industrial enterprises, but ever-present competition between cliques at all levels obstructs monopoly and retards over-centralisation. Though a clique depends on close person-to-person relationships, the whole Japanese nation has grown over the years into a single clique, a 'clan' which separates its citizens from all non-Japanese. The clan incorporates many small cliques which may be called 'cells' and 'fraternities'.

In the West the family takes priority. It is of very great importance in Japan also, but the Japanese have a second family at work. For many Japanese bread-winners the source of income takes precedence over the home. Of the many self-contained cells and fraternities that are loosely-knit into the Japanese national clan, all are subordinate to those based on places-of-work, the direct descendants of extended-households and still the foundation stones of the social system. The social structure has retained a communal organisation.

The basic unit of Japan through historic times has been the household 'extended' within its tight walls to include distantly related kin and non-relatives as well as immediate family members, all living in close proximity as a united family, working as a productive unit with an established hierarchy. Inheritance was usually from father to eldest son, but the extended-family adopted and promoted a suitable outsider if he was felt to be more capable than the blood-relative nearer in succession. To ensure the desired succession, adoption has been, and still is, common. I can count dozens of instances I know of personally. Recently a good friend who inherited his family soy-bean sauce business adopted a son to carry it on. This 'father' had been editor of a famous English language newspaper. He continues literary work in the English language while having to devote much of his time to making soy sauce.

Daughters, when they married, became part of their husbands' households unless the husband was adopted by the daughter's family and, to join her, severed his ties with his parent's household. Although close links were often maintained with close relatives who left to live under different roofs, they became 'outsiders'. Whatever the blood-ties, organisation within an extended-household was as close as that between parents and their children. Filial duty was primary, the individual secondary to the household under the strict rule of a head, the 'father'. Survival depended on giving priority to the household and keeping blood-ties, though strong, in second place.

The Japanese extended-household, nurtured in a rice-farming community, is no longer universal. Domination by family heads, expulsion from the community and other communal forms of compulsion are no longer as rigid as they used to be. In the countryside forestry workers now organise in trade unions, but agriculture was the nation's backbone only a generation ago and the influence of the extended-family remains ingrained in today's social attitudes.

Despite the movement of labour from the land to the factory, the extended-houshold mentality has hardly been disturbed. The male income earner, his family living in a small house or apartment, often provided by his employers, has switched his allegiance from the extended-household of the farm village to dependence on his employer and to a personalised association with his intimates at his place-of-work in the city.

The affluence of the last decades allows more time to family life and leisure activities. It has changed the priorities of the present generation, but erosion of the place-of-work fraternity has not reached significant proportions. While the individual's closest ties are with his primary fraternity he may, of course, have family, friends and acquaintances outside it, but these relationships are still secondary. Family and leisure play a growing part, but they are not the motive power of the Japanese culture.

It has been said that each Japanese lives within a series of three circles, but the definition of these circles is not unanimous. I suggest that the inner circle is a cell confined to a very small number of intimates who meet constantly and depend on each other implicitly. Each cell is part of a larger organisation which may be likened to a fraternity which gives coherence and strength to the cells it binds together. Each individual relies on his fraternity, although his prime loyalty is to his cell. The fraternities and their cells are bounded within a third-circle, the nation. Beyond each circle, at each level, all other people are outsiders.

'CELLS'

The term cell describes small groups of intimates within larger organisations in the sense that cells of the body link together to form a whole, but the word is not inappropriate if also thought of as imposing the confines of a prison cell. These small, informal but firmly fettered units of about five to twelve persons who meet one another constantly give unity and cohesion to the larger fraternities within which they are sealed.

Japanese individuals work within their cells and rarely cross boundaries to form horizontal associations with outsiders of their status level. Horizontal connections are secondary in the power structure because of the clear distinctions between insiders and outsiders.

The small cells within large place-of-work fraternities are usually but not always the group who work together in a sub-section. The members of some cells may be juniors, scattered in different parts of a large organisation, clustered around a senior quite high up in the hierarchy. He selects his flock, one by one, from new entrants, probably youngsters from his old university. The senior will establish close personal relationship with each of his chosen juniors, encourage them and evaluate their capabilities. The fortunate members of these cells, transferred from one department to another during the course of their training, will keep more close personal contact with the senior who has chosen them than with the sections in which they are working. During their early apprenticeship their immediate chiefs, perhaps stuck in low-level sections, may be jealous of those juniors who they anticipate will, in due course, be promoted to rank higher than theirs.

Each cell competes with other cells and keeps its peers at arm's length, but the tight personal affiliations within each holds together its large fraternity. Rivalries between cells are counteracted by overall fraternal loyalties, the influence of belongingness within the frame of the fraternity, and by rule from above as is normal in all large organisations everywhere.

If the export department of a very large trading company needs legal advice it must, of course, refer to the legal department of the company, but it acts as though consulting an outsider. It takes guidance from (and entertains) the other department in just that way.

A popular cliché that Japanese society is vertically structured contains some truth but it can mislead. Just as in feudal England of earlier times the Japanese family hierarchy has been vertical. The elder brother outranked the second. They were not equals. Primogeniture was legally abolished by revision of the Civil Code after the Pacific War and there is now a tendency to avoid it in the family. In all advanced industrial countries every business is controlled vertically, probably even more firmly than Japanese enterprises which are less monolithically governed with all power at the top. However, while power is vertical as in other countries there is no state body with centralised power to control a 'Japan Incorporated'. The term 'vertical' distorts as a one-word description of Japanese society. Another mis-label, 'multi-layered', gives an impression of horizontal divisions. 'Vertical slices' may be more appropriate, but both images hide the cellular structure which gives life to the fraternities that collectively shape Japan's destiny. In contrast to Western society, Japan is 'non-horizontal', but 'cellular' with vertical hierarchies within and between the cells is a more accurate description.

'FRATERNITIES'

Within the all-embracing national clique small cells unite within larger cliques which act as fraternities. Fraternities of all sorts abound. They are the social system. Until very recently each Japanese has had little alternative but to spend or try to spend his or her life as a member of a cell in a fraternity. Each demands the individual's total commitment and loyalty if he or she is to enjoy its support and to be rewarded with the satisfaction and benefits of belonging. Communal co-operation, confined to fraternity members, is accepted automatically and implicitly. Each individual identifies himself closely with the fraternity's goals. What would be private matters in foreign societies are communal enterprises in Japan. Individuals may lose their fraternal privileges if, as some do, they choose to stay outside the cliques their fellows accept as part of their lives.

The degree of close association, the exclusivity, even the ritual associated with fraternities in the West, all fit, broadly and not inaccurately, the Japanese scene. There is only one distinction. Western fraternities, corporations and societies are bound by formalised and often iron-clad rules. Japanese fraternities, no less strict in their demands on their members and the exclusion of non-members, also have their rules which may be lengthy and binding but are rarely stated in words which do not leave room for alternative interpretations. In changed situations there can be major variations in the way the rules are applied. The Japanese govern themselves and their members by mutual dependence, obligations, loyalties and incentives through intense person-to-person association. They are living organisms, families without blood-ties, controlled by case-by-case decisions which can by-pass hard and fast constitutions.

In every country people cluster in groups – professional associations, trade unions, clubs and societies but in Japan freedom to move from one clique to another is so restricted that an overriding need for fraternity membership far exceeds the same impulse elsewhere. The barriers between the independent fraternities, and even between the cells within them, are so strong that intermediaries are frequently necessary to perform formal introductions or to smooth frictions.

Quite recently, to reach a compromise between conflicting elements within my company, a senior ex-staff member was brought back to assist in a settlement that saved everyone's face. He achieved a compromise satisfactory to both sides, though privately he expressed displeasure that he had not been consulted before the situation had reached the deadlock that he resolved.

The Japanese compete between themselves strenuously but not openly. They discourage aggressive factional competition within their fraternities, but competition between fraternities stimulates each towards internal unity and its own preservation. The economy thrives on it. Those in the same field duplicate the activities of their most successful competitors. Each tries to overcome its rivals by doing the same thing. In commerce, education, and the bureaucracy, just as in olden days between extended-households and religious groups, the closer the fraternities' activities the more strenuously they contend. The leadership is concerned with the profitability of its own fraternity when deciding to compete or to co-operate with other fraternities, the bureaucracy and the State.

Similarities between Japanese and contemporary religious cults in the West should be neither overstressed nor overlooked. The 'People's Temple' cultists who committed mass suicide in Guyana in 1978 took dramatic action to terminate their fraternity. Other cults still continue actively. Against the erosion of family life, coupled with the intense competition to survive financially in the Western world, these cults offer caring involvement, devoid of competition. The appeal of the Western cults corresponds with the advantages given by Japanese cliques – cells and fraternities which function as all-inclusive welfare communes.

'THE CLAN'

The most important feature of Japan's culture is the solid backing of every Japanese for his country. In all contacts with the outside world there is a single, overriding policy, 'Of Japan, by Japan, for Japan'.

The term 'clan' seems to be a meaningful designation for the Japanese nation. That a clan is usually a great family united against outsiders fits the Japanese notion of their whole nation having a common genealogical descent and their continuing exclusivity against non-Japanese. The custom of adoption to perpetuate family names and to hold property has minimised any belief that a family, or clan, must be limited to blood relatives. The designation 'clan' seems more appropriate for a large advanced industrial nation than 'tribe', an alternative term used by Gregory Clark. Both words emphasise how much today's Japan has in common with mankind's earliest societies.

Within clans person-to-person, human relations are of prime importance. They exclude outsiders and give priority to members and unite them for mutual protection. Religions, myths, customs and rituals sustain established rules of morality and behaviour. In Japan before the fifth century the leaders of a number of clans had assumed religious functions, each closely associated with a particular deity. The strongest chieftain, claiming descent from the Sun Goddess, unified the country by military and diplomatic actions under what became imperial leadership. A mythical variation of Japan's prehistory traces the imperial line as undisputed rulers descended directly from the gods. The myth was accepted throughout the land until the end of the Pacific War. Even now, a little less positively, this account of the origin of the leading family, and of the national clan, still persists.

Japanese mythology, with earthy, personalised gods, had set an example for rule by consensus. The gods, it is recorded, met in divine assembly 'in the bed of a river' to achieve harmony and concord. Their precedent was followed by early rulers when they created a centralised government.

Prince Shotoku laid it down in AD 604 that, 'Decisions of important matters should generally not be made by one person alone. They should be discussed with many others . . . to arrive at the right conclusion.' The Taika Reforms, fifty years later, followed the same road and insisted that policy should not be made by the monarch alone.

Not very long ago the rulers of Meiji Japan consolidated their country against outsiders. At this time, the 1870s, the Chinese considered themselves immeasurably superior to all other nations. They made no effort to study the industrial strength of the West nor to learn from it. The foreigners' armed might took possession of parts of China. The Japanese, in similar danger, had been compelled to accept 'Unequal' Treaties which limited Japan's autonomy and gave privileges to aliens. As one way to persuade the aliens to treat them as equals the Prime Minister (Hakubun Ito) and the Foreign Minister (Kaoru Inoue) forced the élite of Japan to wear European clothes, to learn Western dancing and to attend formal European-style balls. Try to image yourself wearing what would seem to be fancy dress and to prance about with 'uncivilized' people to win their favour. The Japanese swallowed their pride in the national interest and achieved their end. The 'Unequal' Treaties were superseded and the Japanese clan regained cliquish independence.

Citizens of all countries may be, quite rightly, proud of their native lands but native cohesion is carried to an extreme in Japan. We aliens have feelings of national patriotism of which we become very conscious when we live or travel outside our native lands, but in peace time a dramatic difference exists btween the degree to which our patriotism influences our decisions and the priorities the Japanese take for granted.

4 Outsiders

JAPANESE OUTSIDERS

Exclusive, self-contained cliques automatically create outsiders. The stronger the consolidation within the fraternities and their cells, the higher the barriers that exclude all others. Distinctions between insiders and outsiders are found in all countries, but in Japan the cleavage is sharp. It permeates and dominates everyone's life. High walls have been erected by intimate human relations which demand an absolute dependence on close associates who protect each other communally and remain aloof from outsiders. Rigid divisions between insiders and outsiders account for the greatest divergence between the Japanese culture and all others.

Foreigners are, of course, automatically outsiders but so also, except within their own tightly self-centred cliques, Japanese are outsiders to one another. Each is so fully occupied within the security of his own cell and fraternity he has little time for those outside it and may not know how to cope with them. Although he is very well informed about his own fraternity and those in competition, his concerns rarely extend further. Within his clique he gains comfort and confidence. Exposed to those outside his communal circle he is self-conscious and worried by lack of knowledge and what other persons may think of him. He derives little satisfaction from being conspicuous.

Hiromi Kiyokawa resident of the sleepy little town of Kanae in Nagano-ken, a 36-year old bachelor office worker, won 10 million yen in the 1978 national year-end lottery and became an instant celebrity and a source of envy when news of his win spread in the district. At first he hoped to buy a home of his own, but people gossiped about his instant wealth and tension developed and some people even refused to speak to him. On reporting to work at the end of the New Year holidays he burned the winning ticket in front of his colleagues, who tried in vain to stop him.

A Shimonoseki company employee who literally fished up a bag of gold abandoned all claim to the booty – valued at almost 50 million yen. Kazue Uemura, 43, was fishing for squid in Shimonoseki harbour when his line struck a snag. After probing the seabed with an iron pole, Uemura pulled up a bundle which contained 21 gold bars. He took the ingots to the Shimonoseki police who suspected they were contraband but no conclusive evidence came to light and the ingots were handed over to Shimonoseki City authorities to await a claimant. As no one came forward to claim the gold within six and a half months, Uemura had finder's right to the treasure. However, Uemura formally renounced all claim to the gold. 'From the time I fished it up, I've been plagued with nasty phone calls asking what I'm going to do with all that gold,' he said afterwards. 'After talking with my family and friends I decided I would be better off without it.' The gold bars reverted to the state.

(Uemura's example was not followed a year later by Akio Hamamoto another fishmerman in the same area who found gold in a similar way. He was given it by the police when no owner claimed it within the legal time limit.)

Each individual becomes enmeshed with those close to him through mutually understood feelings and customs, well established but unwritten. He has great difficulty in communicating with fellow citizens who are not personal acquaintances. It is not thought to be hypocritical to behave with constraint towards outsiders and wilfully with insiders. Three situations have always to be considered: intimate ones between insiders; open formal ones between insiders and outsiders; and secret, hidden action by insiders against outsiders.

It is appropriate, as glaring examples of the barriers between the Japanese, to point out that whole fraternities of racially pure Japanese are treated as outsiders. At least 1 per cent of the population (1.2 million according to census figures but some say there may be 3 million) are descendants of people who had the task of disposing of dead animals and people, of guarding and executing criminals, of tanning leather and of other work considered to be unclean. In 1871 the Meiji government declared these outcasts to be equals, but few social, economic or administrative measures were taken to implement the law. Before taking decisions many prospective employers and parents of those wishing to wed still study family records which, in Japan, must be registered with the local government and open to the public. The outcasts remain a separate and under-privileged community within the clan.

Another 'outside' group of fraternities of pure-blood Japanese, the criminal gangs, have their recognised niche. To the extent that they are less easily identified by family registers, they are less of outsiders than the outcasts. The gangs have used the old traditions and still universal fraternal practices to give themselves a false aura of respectability. They monopolise such shady businesses as gambling, prostitution and the smuggling of revolvers. Recently, they have engaged in drug peddling.

Most gangsters are drop-outs from school and from society who feel themselves unwanted except by their boss. Traditionally, but nowadays not always, they spend years of apprenticeship living in the boss's house and performing chores for him. They pledge loyalty to him and respect his personality and his ability to support them financially. Most gangsters display intensely nationalistic feelings.

The police have seemed to prefer to deal with boss-controlled groups of gangsters rather than undisciplined, individual criminals. However, recent crack-downs indicate that the police now fear the syndicates have become too influential, and the drug trade a menace. Although criminal offences are growing rather than diminishing in recent years, Tokyo boasts of the lowest crime rate of any large city in the world. It would seem that the tolerance of the police has worked despite the very large numbers of known gangs and gangsters.

To revert to the general attitude towards outsiders, other sections of the Japanese population put themselves beyond the pale. Students who show the enterprise to continue their post-graduate studies abroad before seeking employment stand against the system and have trouble finding jobs on their return to Japan. The four years they may have spent in earning a Ph.D. is no merit. Employers are concerned that such young men will not fit easily into the standard training system. If they overcome 'the taint of foreign influence' their salary and seniority start on the level of younger, less qualified men commencing work straight from their Japanese universities.

The experience of a friend, an English language broadcaster in the Japan Broadcasting Corporation (NHK), illustrates the practical significance of these strict rules. His high qualifications and exceptional linguistic ability gained him a British Council scholarship to the University of London and NHK granted him leave of absence. On his return he found that he had forfeited salary increases and seniority for the two years he had been absent. His higher qualifications and his greater ability as the result of his very successful studies abroad were ignored completely. Men who had joined NHK when he did were now his seniors and receiving higher salaries. Even men who had joined the year after him had become his seniors during his absence. He left NHK and is now a professor in a British University teaching British (and foreign) students to speak better English!

It has been said in a symposium on the subject that 90 per cent of young employees of large Japanese firms are reluctant to accept posting overseas. On their return they anticipate that they would have to forget or conceal anything they had learned from their experiences in foreign cultures and to face a lack of trust, reduced status and responsibility while they were reintegrated socially and they 're-learned to be proper Japanese'.

ALIEN OUTSIDERS

With rare exceptions all persons not born in Japan of Japanese parents are aliens to all Japanese at all times and are outside the Japanese communal network to an extent that we Westerners, who accept and often pay little heed to the foreignness of our neighbours in our own countries, may have difficulty in fully comprehending. Second-generation Japanese born outside Japan, frequently less acceptable to Japanese than white or brown-skinned persons, are also aliens to them. The second-generation often suffers the worst of both worlds.

Takie Lebra and others have written that Japanese expect their fellow countrymen to behave like Japanese, that overseas Japanese may be ridiculed and distrusted, and that foreigners are expected to retain their national identities no matter how immersed they may be in Japanese culture.

The clannishness of the Japanese is still carried to great lengths. One of the world's most advanced industrial nations in this day and age has preserved, basically unchanged from 'time immemorial', a person-to-person communal structure which cannot accommodate outsiders.

'Japan's Nationality Law is a left-over from the feudal age of samurai and harakiri,' said socialist Dietwoman Takako Doi (now leader of the Socialist party) on 12 March 1980. She insisted that to improve the law was not a technical problem but required a change in deeply rooted traditional Japanese ways of thinking. She added that 'The Japanese government considers residence and nationality status not as fundamental human rights but as privileges the government metes out.' The Nationality Law has been amended recently but the changes are far from being all-embracing. There are two rigidly different administrative systems, one for Japanese and one for foreigners, as best exemplified by the government's insistence that foreigners must be fingerprinted.

It has been said that Japan ignores the outside world, but is very conscious of it. To keep reminding ourselves that the Japanese are extremely aware that we are aliens brings us closer to mutual understanding. Their attitude towards foreigners is revealed in many ways.

In November 1980 a 41-year-old scientist who, in 1972, had earned his doctor's degree in engineering from Osaka University was arrested for illegal entry into Japan at the age of 10, with his mother, nearly 30 years earlier. Dr Kim se Chang had been using an Alien Registration Card which had been bought for him by his Korean father in 1954 and which he had renewed every three years thereafter. He taught at the Osaka Institute of Technology from 1975 in which year he attended an international symposium in engineering in Algeria and he had also established an enterprise to sell technology. It must be added that the Osaka Summary Court imposed a very lenient fine (Y30 000).

After more than thirty years in Japan I still must, every three (now five) years, attend the Tokyo Immigration Office to re-register as an alien resident and obtain an extension of my visa to be allowed to remain in Japan. (Recently the law has permitted me to become a 'resident alien'. To obtain this status I would have to ask two Japanese friends to be my guarantors, an obligation I am reluctant to incur. I would still have to carry an Alien Registration Certificate and would still have to obtain an exit and re-entry visa each time I left Japan.) On the occasion before last I filled in and presented the form of application for visa extension at the Immigration Office. The officials shelved it until they received once more a letter from my employer (my own company) that it would employ me for another three years, together with copies of my tax returns (national and local), my 'employer's' certificate of company registration and latest balance sheet and profit and loss account, and its undertaking of responsibility for my debts and my good behaviour and the payment of my fare should I be required to leave Japan. For the most recent extension of my visa I had all the papers prepared and, with my signature, submitted by the general manager of my company. The Immigration Office refused to accept them unless I presented them personally.

In 1979 my sharebrokers were told that my name had to come off the register of a public Japanese company even though I had been registered as a shareholder for several years. Long residence and regular payment of taxes in Japan were rejected as immaterial when my sharebroker tried to insist that I was not an overseas investor.

Every foreign resident must at all times carry his or her Alien Registration Certificate. It is made of paper, not plastic. Recently a policeman challenged my blonde, English wife when, dripping and without hers, she swam ashore a quarter of a mile from our seaside house.

In mid-1979 Japan signed an International Covenant on Human Rights. To put this international understanding into effect, one act should have been to withdraw the regulations which enforce the carrying of Alien Registration Certificates. The government has been silent as to its intentions. Since 1982 a number of foreign residents have refused to be fingerprinted on the grounds that this violated basic human rights. The Justice Ministry has made it clear that fingerprinting of foreigners is mandatory. It has refused to allow an exit and re-entry permit to objectors and has taken legal action against the offenders.

In fairness it should be added that the House of Representatives has recently passed a Bill to amend the Alien Registration Law to enable foreigners to reside in Japan for 90, instead of 60 days, without being registered; to permit delays in making some changes in their certificates until they are due for renewal; and to permit a foreigner departing with a re-entry permit to carry his certificate instead of surrendering it on leaving and having to retrieve it on return.

In October 1978 the Supreme Court ruled that it was not unconstitutional for the Minister of Justice to refuse to extend an alien resident's visa if he engaged in political activities while in Japan. The decision, after years of litigation, was against an American teacher, Ronald A. MacLean, who in 1969 and 1970 had been active in opposing his country's war in Vietnam and the US–Japan Security treaty. The ruling was that the human rights section of the Constitution allowed aliens residing in Japan freedom of political activity, but this freedom did not prevent the Justice Minister from refusing to extend their permit to live in Japan.

In late 1980 an alien teacher of English at a small school in Japan wished to move to another school which had offered him a better position. The legal advice he received was that, even though his visa had not expired and he wished to continue in the same work, he had to obtain the approval of the immigration authorities before making the change. For him to have received his visa his present employer had had to guarantee his living expenses and his return airfare from Japan. His new employer would have to give similar guarantees and to submit a copy of his new employment contract setting out salary, working hours and job description. The new employer would additionally have to submit the reasons for hiring, the employer's current commercial registration and tax returns. The teacher would also have to present to the authorities a certificate of income tax withheld from his salary by the previous employer and a retirement certificate from his previous employer to the effect that he was resigning voluntarily. (Should the previous employer refuse to write such a statement an explanation of why it was not available might suffice.) Finally, the immigration officials could request a statement of his reason for changing his job.

In 1980, to become an official of the Japan Sumo Association, a position he earned by creating records as a sumo wrestler, Jesse Kuhaulua (known to millions of sumo fans as Takamiyama – his wrestling name) had to become a naturalised Japanese citizen. He became Daigoro Watanabe.

Aliens may become naturalised Japanese, but the authorities impose strict and time-consuming procedures. One of the very few aliens I know who has become a Japanese citizen had to make 34 trips to the Ministry of Justice over a period of 18 months. He made ten trips before he was even given a list of the documents required to make an application. Every visit involved at least a half day of his time. He felt that the authorities were testing the sincerity of his desire by maximising the waste of time and the loss of income he experienced.

Alien companies may now more easily than in the past obtain permission to carry on business in Japan but it is still common parlance to label them as 'invaders'. Even though aliens pay the same taxes as Japanese, rarely do resident aliens receive even a modest portion of the various social welfare benefits available to Japanese nationals. However, a big concession was made in line with the Human Rights Convenant. It was announced in February 1980 that foreign residents might be permitted to seek housing loans and seek public apartments built by the Japan Housing Corporation. Some discrimination against foreigners is, therefore, being reduced but high barriers remain.

The Japanese implicit assumption of separateness, cultural and racial, is a fact of everyday existence the awareness of which diminishes only in rare cases between aliens and Japanese who have lived closely over a long period of years. Within limits, this attitude of separateness, however, may not exist in the daily life of a Caucasian alien among Japanese who have accepted him, or her, as part of their community.

For a number of years my family has had a beach house in a small village with no foreign neighbours for a mile or more in any direction. Despite our 'red hair' we are accepted as part of the village life to such an extent that we feel that even the children no longer notice our blonde colouring.

Although kept in a separate category, and despite irritations, the Caucasian alien, who lives within the limits of Japanese law and customs, is treated well. He or she is given cordial helpfulness and distinctive status which, for most, is very favourable.

On the other hand, at mandatory visits to their local Ward offices to obtain their Alien Registration Certificates or have them altered, Caucasians never cease to be surprised how many people in the queues could easily be mistaken for Japanese. The overwhelming majority of aliens are Koreans and the position of Oriental aliens is more difficult than that of Caucasians.

> Of about 750 000 alien residents in Japan about 650 000 are ethnic Koreans. Most, about 70 per cent of the Koreans, are children or grand-children of men who, during the 36-year Japanese colonial rule of the Korean Peninsula that ended in 1945, were forcibly transferred to Japan as cheap labour for Japanese coal mines, construction sites, shipyards and other places of work, or men who served in the Japanese Imperial Army. Koreans in Japan are classified into three groups. About 65 per cent have been granted permanent resident status under a 1965 Tokyo–Seoul agreement which made them nationals of South Korea. Then there are more than 10 0000 who lived in Japan before 1952 but refused to acquire South Korean nationality. The third group of more than 10 0000 were born to the second group. They must apply for Justice Ministry approval for renewal of their residence permits every five (it was three) years.
>
> It is said that of about 10 000 Korean school-leavers each year only one out of ten gets a job with a Japanese company. About half find work in the Korean business community in Japan, leaving about 4000 each year who cannot find regular work. While Koreans pay taxes as the Japanese, they are excluded from many classifications of social welfare.

Japanese nationalism since 1945 has been very evident in trade but territorially has been channelled along less aggressive lines. The urge for more territory – Okinawa, the 'Northern Islands' and the Sankaku Islands – may be deemed aggressive, but there has been resistance to the building up of military ('Self Defence') forces.

The value to themselves of integrating Japan with the world will be clear to the Japanese if they look closely at their own quite recent history. Little more than a hundred years ago Japan was a conglomeration of nearly three hundred domains, each restricted and controlled by the central authority, the Tokugawa government in Tokyo. Each had its distinctive customs and each managed its own affairs after its own fashion. Each domain had a great deal in common but, at the end of the nineteenth century, one well-known Japanese statesman, Yukio Ozaki, said categorically that his country had been 'a grouping of independent states' during his youth fifty years earlier. The centralisation of Japan into a single nation is a comparatively recent accomplishment and the statesmen who achieved it in such a short time did so because they clearly saw the advantages to their country. With such a successful example within their own land, the Japanese could be very strong partners in breaking down world barriers, but to do so the deep divisions between Japanese and aliens and also between 'insiders' and 'outsiders' within Japan would have to be reduced.

PUBLIC SPIRIT

Japanese sensitivity must be contrasted with what, to the foreigner, are extremes of insensitivity. The Japanese have a highly developed eye for beauty and an equal ability to ignore what they do not want to see. Their oblivion to the black-hooded stage-hands who move the props 'unobserved' on the kabuki stage may be paralleled in the West by our 'suspension of disbelief' at our theatres, but in Japan there is a much wider and generally accepted distinction between things which are 'inside' and those which lie 'outside' in the public domain. Japanese feel little social responsibility outside their communal cliques and a determined lack of awareness of 'outside' things.

Public transport has developed since the traditional rules were established. Between the rigid conformity expected in the home and the place of work, a Japanese worker mixes with outsiders each morning and evening on his long journey by public transport. Free from obligations to people he knows, he can elbow his way to be first on to a train. He can dive for and retain a seat without thought for older and infirm fellow passengers. If they can't fight their way to seats they must strap-hang. They are outsiders with no influence on his position with his inner circle. Behaviour during the rush hour, the pushing and shoving, the abandonment of politeness, of good manners, of dignity, shock foreigners. One trip by any Japanese city railway at any rush hour demonstrates vividly that politeness is not customary amongst strangers (outsiders).

To the foreigners who work with them, Japanese people seem obsessed with the quiet but wholehearted pursuit of material, financial, professional and social success, to a primary concern with the here and now. In their daily lives they combine with aesthetic appreciation a keen awareness of material things. They are lovers of and despoilers of nature. Profit comes before the preservation of nature which is appreciated on a personal, not yet a public level.

The killing of shoals of dolphins by the fishermen at Iki in 1978 and again in 1980 caused world-wide storms of protest which many Japanese found difficult to comprehend. To the fishermen concerned with feeding their own families, and to a majority of their countrymen, ecology came after livelihood was assured. The dolphins were eating the commercial catch.

The indiscriminately jettisoned litter that so often offends the eye in places of public recreation – beaches, mountains and parks everywhere – provokes many aliens. How can people who react rapturously to the sights and sounds of nature accept with tranquility the mounds of rusty cans and other refuse that so distract Westerners and, slightly less displeasing, the electric power lines at scenic resorts that jar the foreign eye?

Not long ago a Prime Minister's Office study concluded: 'Japanese youths have little sense of public duty or social responsibility due to intense competition for university entrance and thence lifetime employment . . . Their abnormal behaviour is an extension of what everyone does – ignore everyone else.'

Public needs not within the normal scope of each clique's activities are usually neglected. Communism is on a personal, not geographic basis. A city or village provides living or working space, but its inhabitants and workers are not concerned with the city or village except for people within their cliques and during local festivals or similar activities. If outsiders are expected to cope with affairs outside the realm of a clique, nothing is done. On the other hand, once a public need is seen, and an organisation set up to handle it, efficient steps will be taken to meet it. Not so long ago Tokyo was a dirty city. Today its general cleanliness is most favourable when compared with conditions in London, New York and other large cities. Although there are still few organisations, other than local governments, coping actively with area related problems, this situation is slowly being tackled.

5 Dependence

DEPENDENCE

It cannot be over-emphasised that the dependence enshrined in each individual's make-up is the taproot of Japanese behaviour. Dependence and conformity have been obligatory when living closely together for countless generations. In houses without private rooms or lockable doors, as exposed as goldfish in bowls, the Japanese have been forced to depend on and submit to one another. Until recently constant exposure to watching eyes have made them dependent, self-conscious perfectionists. Acceptance of communal living has been the normal, unavoidable way of life with each person forced to restrict his, or her, individual emotions and actions.

In any society complete individual freedom of action would reduce social living to a state of anarchy. To avoid chaos and to obtain security we Westerners, though we resent and oppose regulations on principle, tolerate many limitations on our ego. We could not drive a car in safety if there were no rules of the road.

Paradoxically, Japanese roads have been one of the country's havens for the release of egoism. Traffic regulations, being new, lack traditional acceptance and have not always been enforced strictly. The Japanese, never slow to take advantage of unregulated opportunity, have driven with sometimes alarming freedom. The rule that the car that makes the impact is responsible for the accident encourages drivers to cut in front of one another.

Western society thrives on confrontation. We Westerners believe that we must expose and debate our differences to come to understandings. We think of freedom as the right to choose, the absence of enforced obedience and the precedence of the individual over the group coupled with the rights and dignity of man. Nevertheless, in our working lives we follow orders laid down by our superiors. Even at the top level of management, a single person rarely has complete freedom and only a tiny number of people enjoy economic independence. Despite limitations, however, we are brought up with an illusory belief in our independence. Our ego has as goal reduction of the limitations on our freedom. We pride ourselves on the potency of our individual rights and make and break many casual associations. We resent dependency. We feel that the group needs us as much as we need the group. If we are dissatisfied with our positions we can, if it suits us, change to another group.

Japanese, less able to change their fraternities, are unable to accept our faith that the individual is free. They live with communal dependence and make the most of it. It is the overwhelming ingredient shaping their behaviour. To them the individual alone is nobody and becomes somebody by accepting a precisely defined status with his, or her, proper station the foundation of his, or her, existence. Status only exists in relation to the status of others. Japanese know, or feel they know, they are above or below each person they encounter as well as knowing that they are dealing with an insider or an outsider.

Since security comes from holding a recognised place in society they do not think of themselves as 'equal'. They accept restrictions and maximise their egos within clearly defined boundaries. Sharp debate is still shunned, confrontation dreaded. Debate not merely disturbs harmony. It is illogically felt that to disagree with someone's opinion is to cast doubt on his ability and his character, that in an open clash someone must lose face. Go-betweens are used to avoid open conflicts.

Takeo Doi, the eminent Japanese psychiatrist, sees a striking difference between the psychology of the Japanese and of other peoples. He has stated that if a Japanese person acts independently,

> he invites charges of being selfish or wilful . . . The group for him is basically a vital spiritual prop, to be isolated from which would be, more than anything else, to lose his 'self' completely in a way that would be intolerable to him. He is obliged, therefore, to choose to belong to the group even at the cost of temporary obliteration of his self.

Dependence is expressed forcefully by a Japanese word, *amae*, which is matched in Korean but has no simple equivalent in the English language. It describes the feelings of the infant at the breast towards its mother – the dependence, the gratification, the belongingness, the desire for love, the emotional expectations, the unwillingness to break the bond and to fend for itself in the wider world. *Amae* permits self-indulgence and preserves an indifference to the claims of others.

Language reflects and transmits a culture and gives a key to differences between cultures. *Amae*, far from being an isolated term, is but one of many words in the Japanese language which give expression to the same psychology. Doi quotes and explains the significance of a host of related words none of which has a satisfactory English equivalent.'If there is nothing corresponding to *amae* in the languages of the West,' he writes, 'one must conclude that there is an obvious difference between Westerners and Japanese in their views of the world and their apprehension of reality . . . In terms of psychoanalysis it concerns the links between words as such and unconscious psychological processes.'

Doi insists that Japanese people retain through their adult lives the same basic reliance on others that the baby has, and is encouraged to retain, on its mother – a primitive instinct diminished in Western cultures to the extent that mothers train their babies to face a hostile world on their own feet. *Amae* dominates the behaviour of each Japanese and, in consequence, the whole social system. For each person the need for parental approval matures into a need for social approval to avoid the extreme punishment of ostracism for non-conformity. His relationship with his mother broadens quickly into dependence on his family, then progressively through school associations to his place-of-work where he and those close to him are part of a large clique, his key fraternity. Above this he strongly feels that he belongs to the community of all Japanese – the national clan. Along the way he may create, when he marries, his own family alliance and join other cliques such as sports or university clubs or religious groups and he may also make individual friends, Japanese or alien, but the key to his living is long-term communal integration with and dependence on a limited number of close associates.

The extension of *amae* into adult society has led to communal associations with a recognised relationship of the senior, or culturally accepted parent, to his juniors who, without blood-ties, depend on him as his children. The adult Japanese depends on the warmth and approbation of a small clique of his fellows. He accepts their combined authority, expressed through the instructions of his immediate superior, in the same way that he was bound to his mother and his family. Every alliance is sealed from outsiders and exclusive to its members who identify with and dedicate themselves to one another.

Dependence may be satisfying or a constant irritant, or a mixture of both. The rigid ties may sometimes conceal resentment and even hatred. If rejected, or feeling himelf to be rejected, a dependent person is likely to blame the other party and may switch from loyalty to treachery in extreme circumstances. Independence would contradict the insider's desire for belongingness and nullify the empathy each seeks. Unfortunately, dependence on others breeds anxiety, sensitivity to criticism, fear of outsiders and may also lead to irrational collective action.

In 1983 a 'neighbours' trial', as it became known, shook Japanese society. Kikuyo Yamanaka, a house-wife of Suzuka City, a suburb of Nagoya, left her three-year-old, Yasuyuki, to be minded by a neighbour while she went shopping. The child drowned in a nearby reservoir while playing with the neighbour's son. The Yamanakas sued the construction company for not fencing off the reservoir and also the neighbours, Mr and Mrs Kondo, for neglecting to look after Yasuyuki. A court cleared the construction company. It decided that the Yamanakas were 70 per cent responsible for the accident as they had not trained the child to avoid dangerous places and that the neighbours were 30 per cent responsible. The Kondos were ordered to pay 5 260 000 yen. When the court's verdict was announced the Yamanakas were inundated with telephone calls, as many as three hundred in one day, and letters. A typical letter read, 'Are you human beings? Are you Japanese? You are typical post-war demons . . . How dare you make money out of your dead child?' Mr Yasuhiko Yamanaka lost his job. His employers said they disapproved of his 'making money from his child's death'. The Yamanakas were intimidated and withdrew their claim for compensation. The Justice Ministry had to give a public warning that persons found to have attempted to intimidate parties to a court decision would be prosecuted. Perhaps the law will be upheld more rigorously in future but the dependence of the individual on the opinions of the community is still a large part of the social scene.

It would be gross exaggeration, of course, to say that all Japanese are dependent. History is studded with masterless samurai who are followed by their modern equivalents. I know more and more Japanese who behave in a most individualistic way, but the loners are still only a small proportion of their countrymen. The situation is undoubtedly changing. Nuclear families and Western influences are increasing the number of rugged individualists, but at present this new generation has not reached power.

GREGARIOUSNESS

The Japanese individual exists in a network of person-to-person interrelationships with living human beings and is more comfortable doing what others are doing than being conspicuous by acting alone. Although this approach to life is also part of Western living together and, in Japan, there are many exceptions, most Japanese prefer to be in a crowd, to swim at an over-populated beach and to tour with an organised group, preferably of their associates, kept together by following a guide who carries a little flag.

At one time the whole Japanese nation seems to read, watch, talk about and do the same thing. Books become best sellers. Catch phrases take on and become part of popular speech. Almost all of Japan's huge newspapers are similar in layout, content and comment. It is said that Japanese read them less for facts than to know what their fellow countrymen are reading about. Fads and fashions are patronised. Booms which are nation-wide but temporary fade as quickly as they mushroom.

In formal situations, well established ritual decorum is expected. In intimate, person-to-peson gatherings relaxation can be and is encouraged to be total. In between, from time to time, solitary introspection may be indulged. A Japanese may occasionally choose to be alone for self-reflection and to subdue the internal conflicts he must repress to remain in good standing with his intimates, but he does not make solitariness a way of life. Without the presence of others he is more than lonely. He cannot afford to be left out of his clique's activities. He would be deprived of the constant exercise of keeping or improving his place in relation to his associates. While absent from his place-of-work he fears being overlooked.

The total separation occasioned by travel is recognised by ritual and extravagant partings and welcomes-back to symbolise continuing acceptance by the fraternity. The number of participants in these 'ceremonies' reflects the status of the traveller, not the period of the journey. The gatherings may be ridiculously large and time-consuming, but are a function of retaining membership of the fraternity from which the member is excluded as long as he is physically unable to share in the togetherness. Dependence on physical proximity for communication makes correspondence difficult.

Self-discipline would be intolerable were there no compensations. These exist. The inner circle gives a cosy feeling of belongingness and empathy to its members and permits of mutual expectations. Each enjoys constant harmony with his intimates in protecting their and his own welfare. Emotions have to be hidden in normal social intercourse but drunkenness and extremes of sentimentality are permitted outlets in acceptable circumstances. Free behaviour at traditional community festivals follows established rules which mix order and disorder – spontaneous activity accentuated by alcoholic euphoria. Tension is released and high spirits encouraged, the community spirit reinvigorated and order reaffirmed.

Social functions feature heavy drinking and simple games rather than thoughtful discussions. Drunkenness is not appraised as either good or bad in itself. Drinking must be restrained if it in any way interferes with important matters, but to drink with friends is to enhance human relations, something desirable as well as pleasurable. The Japanese are cheerful and happy drinkers who sing sentimental and nostalgic songs till they fall asleep. Drinking may serve to lubricate the wheels of communication and drinking, and even drunkenness, may be a qualification for membership in some fraternities. To promote harmony, Japanese may even pretend to be drunk when at a party with friends.

In 1949, a young foreigner I knew, when driving home sober from his office in Tokyo, hit a pedestrian. The foreigner knew the then prevailing Japanese custom that drunks might be forgiven as they were not in full possession of their faculties. He rushed to the nearest bar and swallowed two double whiskies to be able to plead drunkenness. The law has since been changed. Now it is a serious offence to drive when drunk. A little has been chipped from the tip of this iceberg, but the general attitude towards drunkenness has hardly been dented. Actions committed under the influence of alcohol are still regarded tolerantly provided the drunk is not at the wheel of a car.

The English and, to a lesser extent, American idea of drinking to remain sober, to 'hold one's drink', seems strangely unreasonable to many Japanese who, quite simply, believe that one drinks to get drunk. To be drunk in front of strangers is a matter of indifference, both to the drunk and to his fellow countrymen unfortunate enough to be travelling the same way. Some foreigners in Japan are revolted by the public acceptance of drunks who, though rarely violent, can and do inconvenience strangers by divulging their innermost secrets and by being disgustingly sick in the streets and on public transport.

The *Mainichi Daily News* of 28 December 1978 recorded the scene late one festive night:

> Drunks sat sleeping or strap hanging, ignoring station names. Papers littered the floor and many areas were covered with nauseating vomit. At the terminal station about 70 persons were dozing or lying on the carriage seats. Many were salaried workers in their forties. The railway workers took great pains to help the drunks who had gone past their stations. Some drunks were embarrassed to find themselves at the terminal. Others were angry and had to be forcibly evicted from the train. Some went to sleep on platform benches ignoring the cold and the attendants' concern for them. At the fare adjustment window a long line formed. Some then waited for taxis, others stayed overnight on the station.

In brief, the Japanese, who constantly conform to the will of their associates and the community, have a great need to release their tensions and are quite capable of relaxing more completely than is customary in foreign lands.

Contradictory actions are to be expected from the battle ground of self-control and emotion.

EMOTIONS AND SELF-CONTROL

A mix of emotions and self-control explains Japanese behaviour. Stern and habitual self-mastery that is accounted a virtue and accepted as a necessity in crowded, consensus dominated, everyday life may build up frustrations which are held in bond until they break to the surface with explosive violence. Sudden changes are to be expected from people who hide their strong personal egos under a thick cloak of acquiescence to others. The Japanese have so many obligations and formal social rules to worry about that some live with constant anxiety and tenseness in fear of doing or saying something out of place. Releases are more dramatic than those of persons who habitually exercise less restraint. Rare but violent outbursts of emotion contrast starkly but understandably with passive acceptance and quiet conformity.

> In September 1979 a Japanese tourist in the Philippines was so incensed because his wrist watch had been stolen in his hotel, the Manila Hilton, that he hurled all trays, pillows, sheets, tables, chairs,

a TV set and even a refrigerator out of his eighteenth floor window. The Philippines police said they thought there had been an avalanche and that the tourist would throw himself out after the furniture.

In the Japanese, emotional stimuli overwhelm logical thinking. Feelings, duty and sentiment contrast with the necessity to control emotion. The tea ceremony, flower arrangement and miniature trees are said to epitomise the diversion of emotion into quiet, controlled outlets. Their occasional violent outbursts do not justify our describing the self-restrained Japanese as excessively emotional. At least one serious scholar, Takie Lebra, says that the Japanese are less full-bloodedly emotional than Westerners. By this she does not imply a biological difference but strong, socially imposed self-control over emotions. In response to unexpected, unusual situations, a Japanese exercises stern self-control to make himself inscrutable to mask his or her feelings.

During the Korean War, a few hours before the news became publicly known, I learned that President Truman had dismissed General Douglas MacArthur. To find what the Japanese really thought of the man who had replaced their emperor as God in Occupied Japan, I gave the news face-to-face to a number of my Japanese friends and acquaintances – executives, clerks, secretaries, waiters, waitresses, a lawyer, a doctor. Everyone smiled. None ventured a forthright opinion. I still don't know whether the smiles hid pleasure or sorrow.

It took me a long time to realise that when a Japanese laughs in a situation that would bring forth an opposite emotional reaction in a foreigner, the laughter shows that self-control has broken down. It must not be taken at face value unless we remember that hysterical laughter is not uncommon in the West.

> The crystal goblet broke, the brandy soaked into the Tientsin carpet. The maid who had caused the damage as she reached for my coffee cup laughed while she set about clearing the mess. I had not been in Japan long and had difficulty in checking my anger.

Although the Japanese change their opinions and attitudes frequently, showing volatility that surprises outsiders, their inconsistencies should be described as emotional only if we use the term as the opposite to thoughtful or logical, as meaning non-intellectual rather than reasoned. Disconcerting swings, often illogical to Western eyes, are almost invariably practical reactions to situational changes, and only emotional in that they are not thoughtful reappraisals.

EGOISM

To describe the Japanese as 'dependent-egoists' is to coin a term as contradictory as 'competitive-communism' and equally useful in envisaging Japanese dualities. Having to decide all one's actions to conform with others expands self-consciousness and makes for extreme egoism.

A world of difference separates individualism and egoism. Individualism implies freedom of choice. Egoism develops more self-consciously the more individualism has to be restricted by self-control. The Japanese demonstrate in their daily lives how people can be egoists without being individualists.

To the Japanese, Westerners who indulge full-blooded emotions appear rough and immature. To them individualism suggests selfishness and lack of self-discipline, not the belief in freedom of choice and personal independence that motivates us in the West. The need to belong confines and controls Japanese activities. Conformity creates internal conflicts but these have to be repressed. Their freedom of choice is limited by their current status and circumscribed by an environment of dependence on human relations. To fit into their position demands strong self-control which nourishes egoism.

Confucian principles are anti-individual in opposition to Christianity which teaches the primacy of each person. Though just as self-centred as people the world over, and just as anxious for material benefits, for prestige and for status recognition, a Japanese does not see himself as an independent entity. Acceptance of his position in society need be no sign of weakness or lack of ego. Self-control displays inner strength. To receive respect one must give respect. Discipline is self-imposed, not the dictate of the state.

To conform and still be egoistic is not necessarily contradictory. Players in the best co-ordinated Western football teams receive the cheers of the crowd as much for their integration in the team as for their personal performances. A Japanese satisfies his ego, constrained though it is, by working in a team in harmony with others.

To show seriousness and sincerity, a Japanese making a request of some importance is likely to explain at length to the interviewer his life and personal interests before broaching what it is he wants. A foreign applicant is more likely to state his objective first and then to give his reasons, set out logically, rarely disclosing his feelings on the matter.

A Japanese is strenuously competitive to hold or improve his status and his personal advantage, but rather than push himself and proclaim his ability, he aims to be appreciated by his patient, consistent effort. To achieve his personal goals within the fraternal strait-jacket he constantly assesses immediate experience by intuition and introspection. This has developed admirable traits: patience, determination, perseverance and self-discipline which are forced on the individual when he, or she, joins a group and accepts its authority. The Japanese are as egoistic as all other human beings. They are not individualists, but they are perhaps more egoistic than Westerners since they constantly and self-consciously control their emotions.

6 Rationality

JAPANESE RATIONALITY

'Using thought to analyse and discuss is nothing but the mind of illusion.' So wrote Tesshu Yamaoka, calligrapher and swordsman, a hundred years ago. He still speaks for his countrymen when they place human relations above abstract reasoning, and intuition above logic.

There can be a world of difference between practical (an inclination to action rather than speculation) and rational (a rejection of what cannot be tested by reason). Argument against calling the Japanese irrational could be minimised by using the words illogical or unscientific. The use of the more controversial word with its Western meaning emphasises the distinction from Western thinking. I am writing from the Western 'rational' stance so that we Westerners may see Japan from our point of view and Japanese readers may see themselves through our eyes.

We cannot hope to understand Japanese behaviour if we think of it as rational in the Western meaning of the word. The Japanese are practical, but they do not follow the logic and the ideologies which are guides to conduct in Western nations. They tend to see the immediate situation to the exclusion of logically related things that Westerners try to keep in perspective. They rely on intuition and their feelings to visualise the situation and the person-to-person relationships involved. Without reconciling divergencies they see the immediate or nearest, the most tangible things divorced from past or future causes or effects. They take little account of broad, less concrete factors, abstract or universal theories, or dogmatic guidelines. Problems of everyday relations are settled in terms of human attachments rather than abstract ethical principles. To them, ideas and logic are 'cold'. Loyalty to persons is 'warm'. Some Japanese businessmen say they do not like youths 'crammed with intelligence'.

This is not to imply that we Westerners rely solely on cold, abstract logic in our behaviour. All of us, Japanese and Westerners, have the capacity for logic and for human feelings, for both intellectual and what to Westerners is irrational behaviour. However, while much of the rest of the world divides issues into black and white, the Japanese avoid dichotomies. To them life and death are seen on a single plane, not as opposites. Japanese abhor the absolute. They prefer harmonious relations.

If to be practical is to be rational, then the Japanese are rational and few would dispute the effectiveness of their approach to many problems. It has been said that they go straight to things, their eyes like fingers used to touch and feel things as they are whereas, in the West, our eyes divide reality to look at things in perspective. They govern their behaviour by concentrating on the concrete situation confined to the domain of immediate experience and to the material advantages and disadvantages to the persons involved. They manipulate situations masterfully without attempting to reconcile divergencies or to appraise long-term causes and effects. They are also adept in attuning to the environment and adapting to it whereas Westerners aim to dominate and subdue. The Japanese highly developed ability to assess opportunities and dangers which lie directly ahead can blind them to see clearly beyond the present. They regard the foreigners' attempts to analyse all the implications of a problem as unnatural, impractical and an avoidance of things as they actually are. Their rejection of abstract theory and neglect of universal guide-lines make the Japanese irrational in the eyes of most Westerners.

Some years ago an American friend was staying at a modern Western-style, centrally-heated, air-conditioned, Japanese-owned and managed hotel in Nagoya. One morning he ordered the 740 yen set breakfast but declined a slice of toast. He had chosen poached egg on toast and he was limiting his calorie intake. He was charged 820 yen. Because he had not taken the full set breakfast, the cashier totalled his bill item by item. Both the cashier and the manager, when he was called to restore calm, were convinced that the foreigner's protests were most uncalled for.

'A local power company', and I quote Toyoaki Ikuta in the *Japan Times* of 15 October 1978, 'has conducted an opinion survey among consumers in an effort to gain information to map strategies for a future eventuality of regular periodic power supply cuts resulting from a fuel shortage. One of the questions asked in the survey was: "What would you do if the power supply were cut?" About 40 per cent of the people surveyed answered that since they would have nothing to do in the darkness, they would just lie down on the floor and watch TV . . . I think that what is impeding the correct comprehension of the energy issue in Japan is the lack of rational and relative thinking. For instance, the Japanese think about an issue in terms of balance between cost and benefits when it concerns their own private pocket but when it is affecting the whole society, they cannot think in so rational a manner . . . At the threshold of the 1980s when the energy issue will become more critical, I wonder if Japan will be able to deal with it satisfactorily. Japan might be able to muddle through it but only after bumping its head against a wall. I cross my fingers and pray that our country will not meet a sudden death as a result of this collision with the wall.'

In 1937 one of Japan's most original inventors, Soichiro Honda, creator of motor-cycles, and a young manufacturing engineer at the time, dismissed academic learning with the terse comment, 'If theory leads to invention, all school teachers would be inventors.' However, when he failed to manufacture piston rings of acceptable quality – his were as hard as rocks and equally brittle and inelastic – he had to look for scholarly help. After the professor of engineering to whom he appealed analysed one of his piston-rings and found the steel deficient in silicon, Honda's scorn for theory diminished. He attended engineering classes but only part-time while he continued as a manufacturer. He neither sat exams nor sought a diploma. His interest remained concentrated on the practical.

In dealing with Red Army terrorists who hijacked a Japan Air Lines jetliner in 1977 in India, Prime Minister Fukuda asserted that 'human lives are heavier than earth' to justify the Government's unconditional surrender to the hijackers. Six million dollars ransom was paid without negotiation and the government released nine persons charged with or convicted of such crimes as murder, assault, bombing and robbery. That the Constitution separates the powers of the administration from the judiciary was ignored. The cabinet broke the law which does not permit release of prisoners or those undergoing trial. Sunao Sonoda, then Chief Cabinet Secretary and, a few months later, Minister of Foreign Affairs, explained the rationale for the decision to accept the hijackers' demands: 'As a nation based upon law, order must be maintained to protect the lives and security of the people. Destroying that order with our own hands in the face of violence is an act which is hard to bear but . . . thinking of the lives of the 142 passengers and the 14 crew, one cannot just speak of law and order.'

In explaining and confirming the Western view of the irrationality of his fellow countrymen, the late Hideki Yukawa, Nobel Prize winner, has written in *The Japanese Mind* (edited by Charles A. Moore),

Rationalism is a pattern of thinking which enquires into everything in the background of an ensemble of complementary possibilities. The peculiarity of the Japanese mode of thinking lies in its complete neglect of complementary alternatives. This we may term Japanese irrationalism . . . the irrationalism of the Japanese way of thinking, is so peculiar and contradictory that even a Japanese himself finds it hard to understand . . . .

Japanese thought is concerned mainly about the local and temporary order restricted in space and time. This may be termed for convenience, Japanese rationality . . . . Generally speaking a Japanese is out of his element in long-range and abstract thinking . . . . The Japanese mentality is, in most cases, unfit for abstract thinking and takes interest mainly in tangible things. This is the origin of Japanese excellence in technical art and the fine arts . . . .

The abstract mode of thinking will continue to be foreign to the Japanese. And to them any rational system of thought, generally speaking, will not be more than something mystical, satisfying their intellectual curiosity . . . . In the region of science, the Japanese mentality discussed above is reflected in laying stress on applied science and correspondingly in the negligence of rationalistic, abstract, and fundamental study . . . . Unique in world history is the fact that in a corner of the Orient a distinguishing form of culture has been cultivated.

That the Japanese do not think or act in the same way as Westerners does not mean that their behaviour is better or worse, only that it is different. Western rationality is not the only way to handle problems. Yukawa was in no way negative in his objective analysis. He added,

In the light of the present day world predicament, close examination of the possibilities contained in oriental thought is essential . . . The Oriental has the subtle wisdom to devise comfortable conditions of human living by adapting himself to natural conditions . . . There would seem to be an urgent need for searching out the possible ways in which Japanese cultural elements may contribute to the dissolving of the world-wide predicament of today.

In support of Yukawa, Hajime Nakamura, (also in *The Japanese Mind*) summarises the main features of the Japanese way of thinking as:

1. The acceptance of actuality . . . .
2. Human relationships as of greater importance than the individual . . . emphasis upon hierarchical relations of status . . . abso-

lute obedience to some particular person . . . closed character of sects and cliques . . .
3. Non-rational tendencies: (a) non-logical tendencies; (b) weakness in ability to think in terms of logical consequences;(c) intuitional and emotional tendencies . . . .

He adds,

The Japanese language, so far, has had a structure rather unfit for expressing logical conceptions. The fact that is difficult to make derivatives representing abstract nouns means that it has not been habitual for the Japanese to be aware of the relationals between the universal and the individual in terms of logical thinking . . . . As is shown by the historical development of Japanese thought – the ability to think in terms of abstract universals has not fully developed among the Japanese. They have been rather poor in ordering various phenomena on the basis of universal patterns . . . Japanese expressions are for the most part abundant in aesthetic and emotional feelings . . . Japanese expressions focus the thought and expression of the person on immediate, concrete details of life. This tendency is quite unique to the Japanese. That is why the Japanese way of thinking habitually avoids summations of separate fact into broad statements about whole categories of things, although such abstraction is necessary for logical and scientific thinking.

In opposition to Yukawa and Nakamura, Japanese who claim rationality for themselves and their countrymen reject 'Western duality' in separating subject and object, good and evil, yes and no.

Shosen Miyamoto criticised Yukawa whose presentation quoted above he considered 'inadequate'. Of it Miyamoto wrote, (again in *The Japanese Mind*)

The greatness of Japanese art does not lie merely in 'irrationality' . . . . A certain amount of abstraction and rational thought-process is necessary for the conception and expression of art . . . . This is not mere irrationalism or intuition, but a balanced and exact observation of Nature . . . . [Buddhism has] attain[ed] a level of rational, scientific thought which developed scientists such as Noguchi, Yukawa and others . . . . The Japanese mind has been trained in rational thinking by Buddhism for many centuries . . . . The West lives in a world separated into two terms: subject and object, self and not-self, yes and no, good and evil, right and wrong, true and false. It [Buddhism] is therefore more logical or scientific, where yes cannot be no and no cannot be yes . . . . The mystic has a very concrete and therefore a very positive experience of ultimate reality which cannot be conceptualised under the ordinary rules of logical thinking. Logic, as we understand it, has its limitations.

One more example shows the Japanese viewpoint. Michihiro Matsumoto, authority on *haragei* which will be discussed later, has written,

The word 'information' is *wa-ke* in Japanese. *Wa-ke* can be written with the Chinese characters meaning either 'situation/ circumstances' or 'reason'. In Western business importance is placed on the latter, whereas in Japanese business, importance is placed on the former. In fact, the Japanese are adept at finding a reason in a situation/circumstances. This is the concept of 'a reason beyond reason'. This is not necessarily a rejection of reason but a philosophy which transcends reason.

A sharp perception of 'reality' to the neglect of abstractions can be an admirable trait but, unfortunately, not everyone sees reality as the same thing. We, all of us, tend to see things as we expect or want to see them. The Japanese, since they may ignore cause and effect, establish their view of the reality of a situation as much by intuition and human feelings as by objective observation. For mutual understanding both sides must see the same reality or at least try to see the other's reality.

Superficial appearances loom large. If I entertain a foreigner, he will be concerned with the taste, not the price, so I take him where the food is best. To entertain a senior Japanese, the higher the price the restaurant charges the more effective my hospitality. I must take him to an expensive restaurant even though its food may be mediocre.

Concern for the practical overrules intellectuality. Japanese intellectuals there are but, in the eyes of many Westerners, many of their theories are sweeping and vague and not always based on fact or related to reality. The Japanese need, to which they have been educated, to preserve harmonious human relations retards original thinking and inhibits controversy which in its turn would stimulate intellectual debate.

The Japanese are diligent and extremely good at amassing information and are always making forecasts, estimates and plans, but one plan is often superseded by a later one. In nine years from 1955 the government made not less than ten long-term plans for the economy, each for a period of from five to ten years, but each was scrapped for a new plan after an average of less than three years. This shows a sensible ability to revise as situations change, but also indicates that account may not have been taken of all the alternative possibilities. A flaw can be to neglect all factors.

> On the day Prime Minister Ohira left for a five-day visit to China, the *Asahi Evening News* of Wednesday, 5 December 1979 reported as front page news,

> A Japan–China joint statement to the press, which will be issued in Peking Friday . . . will say Japan and China will co-operate in the economic, cultural and resources-energy fields. Prime Minister Masayoshi Ohira and Chinese Premier Hua Guofeng will express satisfaction with the present shape of Sino-Japanese relations. They will confirm that the Sino-Japanese Treaty of Peace and Friendship is conducive to peace and stability in Asia and the world. The joint statement was put into final shape Wednesday morning. The document will say Ohira has offered Y 50 billion in yen credits in the initial year to help finance six Chinese development projects. It will also quote Ohira as saying Japan will co-operate in a project to build a memorial hospital dedicated to friendship between the peoples of Japan and China. The statement will say Hua has accepted an invitation to make an official visit to Japan in May, 1980. The statement will say the two sides have agreed to hold annual consultations between senior working-level officials of the two countries alternatively in Tokyo and Peking. It will quote Ohira as saying steps are being taken to apply preferential tariffs to Chinese products exported to Japan from April, 1980. Ohira and Hua will express satisfaction that basic agreement has been reached in negotiations for the joint development of oil reserves in Bohei Bay.

A weakness of this 'plan' could have been that it was leaked to the press and published before one head of state had met the other.

An appropriate footnote to Japanese 'rationality' is Japanese reaction to the revelation in June 1982 of the illegal buying, for about US$600 000, of IBM computer secrets by their rivals, two large Japanese companes, Hitachi and Mitsubishi Electric. While the West blamed the Japanese in what appeared to us to be reprehensible activities, the Japanese response was quite different. To them (and I quote an analysis of public opinion by Masaru Ogawa, Executive Director of the America–Japan Society) the American FBI was the culprit in the case because of its 'underhand methods in tracking down the conspiracy'.

It is easy for aliens to say that the Japanese are not governed by Western logic, but we also neglect our logic when it diverges from ideals which we accept without thought as universal truths, and when our ethics or habits conflict with rational action. We engage in business for profit without which the whole of our capitalist system would collapse, but we do not always follow the profit motive through to logical conclusions and we criticise the Japanese when they do.

Western manufacturers do not always charge the highest price the market will pay when supplies are short. We do not insist on cancelling or amending uneconomic contracts. We criticise the Japanese when they keep their factories running by selling 'below the cost of production'. We blame the Japanese for trying to protect their home market for their own makers. (They blame us for not trying hard enough to overcome their clan interests and their materialistic desire to make a profit for themselves.) If we do not run our businesses to maximise profit are we not irrational?

While a high proportion of everyone's actions is swayed by feelings or habit without conscious thought, we Westerners more frequently endeavour to make logical decisions than do the Japanese.

Part III

Continuity and Transmission of an Ancient Social Structure

Part III

Continuity and Transmission of an Ancient Social Structure

7 Tradition

CULTURAL ORIGINS

The young react against tradition, as witness the student riots of 1968, but Japanese society is still in an ancient mould. In primitive communities close human relations were inevitable. Each person depended for survival on co-operation with his fellows. As tribes grew in size each had a leader, or a leadership group of elders, to make and enforce decisions. Hierarchies developed. Twentieth-century Japanese still retain the human relations and hierarchical values of ancient societies. They feel themselves to be part of an exclusive, long-established nation which clearly separates its citizens from those of all other countries. Within their nation they accept their places in complex cliques and hierarchies with mutual dependence, conformity, status leadership and distinctions based on age and sex. Despite plentiful exceptions, most gain greater satisfaction by working together than competing singly as individuals.

Pre-1945 attitudes were explicitly enunciated by the Ministry of Education in 1937 as, 'The harmony of our country is not mechanical cooperation, starting from reason, of equal individuals independent of each other, but the grand harmony which maintains its integrity by proper statuses of individuals within the collectivity and by acts within these statuses.' The nation was then more autocratically controlled than it now is.

How, in today's sophisticated Japan, can we account for the survival of communal, or communistic, characteristics which shaped the structure of ancient societies? The short answer is that the Japanese have never been subjugated by foreign invaders, but other factors could have contributed.

Scholars have advanced many alternative explanations for the origins of Japan's twentieth century culture – severe environment, rice culture, insularity, racial and social homogeneity. Taken separately none appears satisfactory, but all have probably played some part.

That Japanese intense cliquishness has grown out of the battle against the harshness of the physical environment is unconvincing as a single explanation since the same reasoning is used in Japan to

65

account for Western individualism. Also deficient is the proposition that the Japanese are as they are only because of reliance on a wet-paddy, rice economy as distinct from nomadic grazing and hunting or dry agriculture. China, Korea, the Philippines, Indonesia, Thailand and other Asian countries fall into the rice-culture category while their peoples have some essentially non-Japanese characteristics.

The suggestion that today's Japan has a communal civilization because it is an island nation ignores the fact that insularity also moulded the British. In prehistoric times Japan harboured waves of immigrants from the neighbouring Asian landmass and possibly the south. Migrants who came to stay. Japan had intermittent relations with Korea and China for more than a thousand years before her sailors, traders and pirates roamed far and wide in the sixteenth century. For two hundred and sixty years from AD 1600 intercourse with other nations was drastically restricted, though never totally abandoned. Does this interval of partial isolation fully explain a retention of dependence on human relations in contrast to the development of individualism? Insularity may have entrenched racial homogeneity though present-day Japanese do not have a uniform cast of countenance.

National cultural homogeneity is a recent growth. Little more than a hundred years ago the scattered communities were mainly concerned with their regional communal conformity. Centrally controlled police surveillance had enforced a degree of national homogeneity, but Japan was segmented into many self-contained domains separated by restrictions on transport.

Severe environment, rice culture, insularity, racial and social homogeneity have one thing in common. All point to evolutionary development as opposed to dramatic upheavals and, singly or in combination, they confirm the fact that today's Japanese social structure still closely parallels its earliest form.

Excluding young nations whose citizens migrated from countries which had suffered invasions, and excluding its Occupation 1945–52, Japan is unique amongst the large nations of the world in not having been overrun by foreign warriors during the last thousand and more years of recorded history. Civil wars Japan endured in plenty, but victories and defeats were between people with the same social system. Internal wars could have reinforced each person's dependence on the martial strength of his own clique. Death and deprivation hurt the losers, but they were not made slaves to foreigners with entirely different governments. Japan has not suffered the traumatic social and individual repercussions of being overwhelmed by a hostile nation and forced to accept government by people with whom they had nothing in common.

'Human relations' to describe Japanese social intercourse empha-sises positive mutual dependence. Subjugation by alien occupiers of ancestral lands would have destroyed deeply entrenched person-to-person bonds. Even if losers had not been made slaves, the absence of human relations between victors and vanquished would have changed the established system of mutual dependence and would have added impetus to individualism. Nothing happened to the Japanese to uproot their original, communal, human relations, social structure. We Westerners have, of course, human relations with our fellows but we exercise choice and approach our friends and acquaintances as independent individuals, not as intimates to whom we are tied for life by bonds over which we have little control.

Cultural imports through the centuries have always been partial and have not changed the basic social structure, the persisting and informal systems which are the drivng force of Japanese activities. Behaviour and society have been adapted remarkably to Western customs, but only in the superstructure. Gregory Clark's assertion that twentieth-century Japan is still a tribal society cannot be ignored. In my opinion, the ancient communal, or communistic, social structure has been modified only by a greater reliance on the profit motive, which may be abbreviated as 'competition'.

THE RETENTION OF THE OLD

Newcomers to Tokyo invariably comment, when they learn I have been in Japan for more than forty years, 'What great changes you have witnessed.' They are correct. I first saw Tokyo as a desolate wreck – blocks and blocks of burned out ruins and rutted roads with few cars. Squatters lived in shacks. To obtain food for survival, people hawked in the streets possessions that had escaped the fire-bombs. Galloping inflation had reduced to a pittance the wages of those who had work. 'Yes,' I reply. 'There has been great change in living habits and behaviour towards foreigners. Buildings and roads are still being uprooted and rebuilt. There is still constant change, but basic values (the competitive-communist system) have altered surprisingly little.'

Even casual visitors encounter examples of the remarkable ability of the Japanese to accept what they choose of the new while, at the same time, retaining the old. They have a spectacular capacity to make 180° changes if new ideas are approved by consensus. Witness their attitude towards aliens during the ten years before and after 1945. However, though shifts in the international situation may again produce dramatic deviations, the communal roots have so far remained surprisingly static.

The Japanese retain two calendars in everyday life – the Gregorian as in most of the rest of the world and, at the same time, year dates which change with the succession of each new emperor. 1987 is also Showa 62. In 1979 the government, despite opposition, passed legislation giving permanence to the custom. This cumbersome duality can create problems at the time of an emperor's death. William Salter recalls an incident that happened when the present emperor ascended the throne. Misako Sato was born in Kamakura on 3 January 1927. The Taisho era had ended on 25 December 1926 so the birth took place in the second year of the new era, but when Mr Sato went to register it the name of the new era had not been determined. (It was announced in March 1927.) The registrar recorded Misako's birth as 3 January 1926 (Taisho 15th year). The resulting confusion regarding her school entry age made life quite miserable for the poor girl. Salter's example has been challenged as not representative of what happened at the accession of the new emperor, but the experience of the Sato family was probably not an isolated one.

The vast Tokyo metropolis divides its postal system by areas, not by streets. With a population of about twelve million the city has only about thirty named streets. To all Japanese the world-known Tokyo Ginza is a conglomeration of many streets. It has one wide thoroughfare thought of by aliens as the Ginza street.

To visit for the first time an office or factory in Tokyo one of my Japanese staff telephones to learn the way there. He is asked which direction we will come from and what landmarks he knows near our destination. The conversation may last for as long as twenty minutes while my man faithfully lists each corner from the landmarks he knows. Even then, when setting out, I allow an extra fifteen minutes. Almost invariably we have to make many enquiries before we eventually find the place we are looking for. The instructions he has been given are not unlike the following (printed in *Tour Companion* of 30 September 1979) for the benefit of tourists wishing to visit the 'Hundred Flowers Garden' (Hyakka-en) in suburban Tokyo: 'The station of Tamano-i is only three stops, about five minutes in the train, from Asakusa. When you leave the station, turn right and walk to the junction with the main road of Mitokaido. Turn right on it, and walk to the big crossroad of Meiji-dori. A police box is on the near corner. Cross over Meiji-dori and keep going in the original direction. Turn right at the next traffic lights, where there is a noodle shop on the near corner. Again turn right at the first traffic light, this time by a Caltex stand. Take the second turn to the left, by a white building, a short distance down this street. This street ends in a T junction, with a children's playground facing you. The playground occupies a corner site. Turn left, and right, going around the playground. Hyakka-en is next to the playground.'

Traditions of craftsmanship are retained tenaciously by using the old tools, old techniques and old materials. Through the centuries, ruined buildings and sculptures have been, and are, restored as absolute copies of the originals.

Many cars are still blessed at Shinto shrines and carry sacred emblems of pine and bamboo each New Year.

In early times *sumo* wrestling bouts took place in the open air under a canopy to protect the contestants from the worst of the weather. When, to shelter the audience also, the tournaments were held indoors, the traditional canopy, fashioned like the roof of a Shinto shrine supported on four pillars was brought in too. With the advent of television the pillars obstructed the cameras and interfered with the viewers' enjoyment. The Sumo Association objected to the pillars being removed but a typical Japanese compromise was reached. The roof is now suspended from the ceiling – perhaps the only example in the world of a roof being suspended indoors. The result has turned out happily as the roof helps retain the atmosphere of the traditional sport.

Occasionally violent communal behaviour reveals old attitudes. On 10 December 1977 in Yokohama the owner, instructor and members of a martial arts gymnasium beat to death an American youth who had passed by in the street and not shown respect for his seniors. He had to be taught proper manners. The assailants included an employee of the Yokohama City government, an instructor of the National Self-Defence school, and a university student. While playing in the street outside the gynmasium, 15-year-old Michael Frazier (whose mother was Japanese) and a 14 year-old mixed-blood friend were attacked by more than a dozen adult judo experts. Frazier, lying on the ground in the street pretending to be unconscious, was dragged with his friend into the martial arts hall and kicked, punched and hit with a wooden training sword for about twenty minutes. Frazier died of a ruptured liver and the other boy suffered severe injuries. Violence in the street is not part of the Japanese scene. Money was not involved. That the dead boy was American was a coincidence. Similar assaults on juniors by groups of their seniors are commonplace. Deaths of juniors who resist 'test of manhood' or discipline are not infrequent.

If a Japanese Rip van Winkle had drunk himself into a coma in 1867 in a sanctuary within twenty miles of the centre of what is now the wide spread of the Tokyo metropolis, and if he didn't at the sights and sounds immediately drink himself into another century of oblivion, he would on waking find alterations beyond recognition. He would indeed have been fortunate to have slept so long. Wherever he had dossed down, construction of new buildings and new roads must have encroached and the roar of traffic would have woken most sleepers.

Where once had been open fields our Japanese Rip would find multitudes of his countrymen, swordless, wearing Western clothes and with their hair cut in the Western fashion. Warriers would no longer strut the now car-filled streets. Their offspring might be sitting on chairs in offices and homes instead of reclining on grass-mat floors. He would see huge, mechanised factories swallowing hordes of men and women in the morning and disgorging them in the evening to return to their families. But when he became accustomed to the fantastic surface changes, would he find major differences in the social system and behaviour of his fellow countrymen and women?

As a Japanese he would accept surface change as a law of nature. To him the Buddhist concept of universal impermanence, evanescence, and ephemerality – the 'floating world' – would support his belief that everything in life is short-lived. He would take for granted that men must constantly adapt their behaviour to new situations just as they must vary their clothing to adjust to the vagaries of the weather. Alterations in the environment can be blended with an enduring retention of basic habits and beliefs.

He would find that modifications in food, clothing, housing and transportation had altered people. Eating more meat and dairy products and less rice had added inches to the height of many of his countrymen. Better control of diseases and more plentiful food had extended life expectancy.

Rip would also see people living in small apartments and houses, unlike the large extended households of his day though most still with at least some straw-mat floors. Many of his neighbours would be commuting to work in packed trains, the labourers spending their days in factories, wearing Western-style overalls and shoes and their white-collared brothers writing letters or speaking in strange tongues with foreigners at their offices. But a large number of his countrymen when they returned home would be kicking off their shoes in their tiny entry halls, then probably removing their Western suits, their ties, collars and shirts and slipping into one piece, droop-sleeved kimono-type robes – replicas of the garments which had been worn for a thousand years.

In looking for the real Japan, the country that accepts change readily but clings tenaciously to the old, Rip would still enjoy the theatre. Japan, a living museum of theatrical history, still provides ancient rituals unchanged over the centuries. Even in today's Tokyo Rip would find, without difficulty, more than a hundred local festivals during the year. He could visit the old forms of theatre with which he would have been familiar – kabuki, noh, bunraku and, if he wished, modern plays, ballets and operas. He would find old rituals being enacted in exactly the same form as their original productions, some a thousand and more years old. Nowhere else in the world do ancient rituals and the theatrical arts of past ages remain intact and alive on the same scale as in Japan.

If Rip overcame the shock of finding himself an outsider, no longer a member of a clique, and examined carefully his countrymen's behaviour he would probably decide that, while daily lives were not as he had known them, the social structure had remained surprisingly intact despite the transition from an agricultural to an industrial manufacturing economy. He may conclude that the new generation, though it eats differently, clothes differently and even sits and sleeps differently, does not think differently from its forefathers.

The old is perpetuated in childhood training, the language and the old religions. It survives in the Japanese house.

THE JAPANESE HOUSE

Tourists may themselves see something of this persistence of old values. Wherever they stay in Japan, in any city or town, they are likely to find a typical Japanese house within a short distance of their modern, Western-style hotel. It may be partly concealed by a high, solidly built wall and what is in sight may seem similar to a house back home, but the more the tourists learn about it the more differences it will disclose. It can give visual, tangible evidence that Japan's culture differs from that of other nations.

The Western house has been designed by and for independent individuals. Its strong walls exclude visitors as well as intemperate weather. For seclusion, Western family members can lock the doors of their own private rooms. The Western house is described by an architect, Koichi Nagashima, as 'a sort of man-made cave with holes, a strongly enclosed space' and the Japanese house as 'a floating roof, a shelter from the sun unconfined by solid walls with no clear distinction between inside and outside space'. Under its 'floating roof' the Japanese house is essentially one whole space divided by moveable screens, sliding partitions and lightly-made walls as opposed to the Western collection of defined spaces, enclosed rooms.

The Japanese house is protected by high, strong walls along the land boundaries to exclude 'outsiders' but, within the house, behind its sliding shutters, the thin walls and partitions emphasise communal living with open access to all 'insiders', whether or not blood-related. The lack of privacy creates a need for self-control and communal co-operation for all who live in intimate contact.

Until recently the Japanese have not built for permanence. An obvious feature of their wooden houses, the flimsy construction and vulnerability to devastating fires, links with Japanese concentration on the immediate rather than the long-term. They still do not expect their houses to last more than twenty or so years. In this they have the backing of superstition which says that to build for permanence is an outright challenge to the gods and may lead to retribution by them. The most important Shinto shrine, that to the goddess Amaterasu at Ise, is still torn down and replaced with a replica about every twenty years in perpetuation of old beliefs.

Large houses have accommodated the owner's family and all his dependants. The householder who manages a farm or small business may still give place to his employees and their families under his communal roof, and many adults still stay with their own children in their parents' traditional-style homes. Although extended-households are becoming fewer and more and more families now live in their own small houses or apartments, a recent Health and Welfare Ministry estimate is that 70 per cent of elderly people are currently living with their adult children. It predicts a decline to 50 per cent by the year 2000.

The tourists will also see rows and rows of small houses ('rabbit hutches') which have proliferated for individual small families. The old order changes. Some new houses have wooden floors and Western furniture but most are cramped and keep the family intimately close. Change in the traditional form has been minimised and some old features are reproduced even in high-rise blocks of apartments. Neighbourhood Associations play a part in replacing the extended family.

The old Japanese houses which are still to be found evidence a continuity from man's earliest form of social organisation. They physically demonstrate a deep-seated cultural difference between communal living and individual independence. Their high outer walls symbolise the barriers between insiders and outsiders.

ASSIMILATION

In passing we should note that the growth of Japan's highly industrialised and in many sectors superbly efficient twentieth-century society can be reconciled with its retention of a primitive communal culture by a single word, 'assimilation'. By adapting to her needs those features she has chosen from foreign cultures, Japan has stayed with her original, indigenous values while developing and refining them into the organisation of a sophisticated, modern society.

During all her recorded history Japan has been in close touch with advanced civilisations, first the Chinese and Koreans, later the Portuguese and Dutch, then, over the last hundred years, the other Europeans and Americans. The Japanese skill in absorbing new ideas has grown through centuries of practice from the time of the acceptance and adaptation of Buddhism and its fusion with the native Shinto over fourteen hundred years ago, to the recent exploitation of the transistor.

The Japanese, not having been forced to accept the ways of conquerors, have been able to measure new ideas against their existing ones. They have had the option of retaining the old intact or selecting new ideas that suited them. They have consciously chosen from advanced civilisations those innovations that fitted into their established customs. The new has been integrated, almost sneaked in, without confrontation, leaving the established heritage remarkably unscathed.

Societies relying on individualism, which incorporates abstract, intellectual, logical principles, resist outside ideas as threats to their cultural identity. China, a classic example, rejected learning from the West. On the other hand, in a communal society the only threat is to human relations. The Japanese happily digest and are nourished by foreign ideas and technologies while they hold outsiders at arm's length and resist close personal involvement with them.

The exchange of knowledge in the past has been so much in one direction that the Japanese have been charged with being imitators, not innovators. Assimilators is a more cogent appraisal. Imitation without comparison with existing knowledge and adaptation to local experience is unlikely to be productive. Dynamic growth comes from mixing and welding the new with the old. The Japanese have modified and greatly improved much of the technology they have imported. In the major fields of electronics, steel-making, automotive equipment, ship-building, chemicals and electrical machinery much of the imported technology has been used either to produce an entirely new product or process, or one that is sufficiently different to be patentable. The transistor, invented in the Bell laboratories in the United States in the 1950s, was applied to radio by Masaru Ibuka of Sony.

It must not be thought, however, that Japan's ability to absorb and take advantage of new ideas has no flaws. Personal relations are sacrosanct. Even in the sciences and industry senior professors and top managers have often achieved their positions as much by their number of years in the university or the company as by their personal ability. Juniors may not be encouraged to display their ability or to advocate new ideas. Individual creativity may be frowned on. Nevertheless, that which is new is accepted and improved upon provided human relations are not ruffled.

Recently the Japanese have been exporting their knowledge as well as their products. The United States Department of Transport now negotiates with the Japan Railways for 'bullet' train knowhow and US Steel with Japanese steelmakers for their advanced technology. Japan's impact on the might of European and American industries and the value of her techniques are seen in the steady stream of supplicants now visiting Japan to ask her to set up factories on their soil. Yet another flood of overseas manufacturers' representatives studies the Japanese 'mysteries' of lifetime employment, productivity and quality control, or to purchase licences for the rights to Japanese patented processes.

All people learn from their neighbours. Cultural and economic borrowing is a very civilised custom that has advanced all countries. The Japanese have duplicated the imitativeness of other races by absorbing new ideas within the framework of their established values, customs and knowledge. Industries now invest heavily in their own research and development. The charge of being imitators is heard less frequently than in the past.

8 Hierarchy

HIERARCHY

In Japan hierarchy is no abstract term. It is a very real fact of life which overrides and bypasses the 'class' divisions of Western industrialised countries. As Westerners believe in equality and free enterprise, so Japanese believe in holding their proper station. Every person's status is clearly defined and acknowledged by all he meets. Minute gradings of rank are carefully distinguished so that everyone is able to relate his position to those with whom he comes in contact. Visiting cards, a major tool of the system, give not only names, addresses and phone numbers but also rank. They show the fraternity the individual belongs to and his status within it. Cards should be exchanged when strangers meet so that each knows the other's position and is then able to behave in accordance with it.

Quite recently, in my company, we found that the English title 'Assistant to the President' translated into a very low rank in Japanese. To show this staff-member's status more accurately on his visiting cards we chose Japanese ideographs which translated into English as 'Manager of the President's Room', a high rank.

Before language was written and information easily dispersed, experience accumulated with those who had lived longest and they were given status. In later centuries Buddhist reverence for ancestors was traditionally combined with Confucian precepts that the older take precedence over the younger. Nowadays rank is still related to age and experience. The date of entering a company, even though the difference may be slight, firmly establishes a person as higher or lower in status during his first five and more years of service in a large organisation. However, even during these early years, juniors who prove to be willing and able to accept responsibility are given the most challenging jobs, and carefully considered rewards within the seniority system are given to the industrious.

Within the hierarchy with its traditional framework, there is intense competition at all levels and at all times. A large company may engage hundreds of new employees each year. All have the seniority of the year they began working, but there has to be a weeding out after the early years and the higher the employee climbs the more acute the struggle. Juniors rarely jump ahead of able seniors, but poor performers get left behind. The longest serving member of a corporation will usually be its titular head but 'lifetime' employment gives no assurance that every employee will rise to be president, or even director, after long years of service. Promotion is within a pyramid-like frame with new recruits at the base and less and less room as the peak of president is reached after thirty and more years of service.

Length of service is not now the criterion for advancement that it was even ten years ago. In new, expanding companies there has at all times been a tendency to promote by ability rather than age and even in old, large companies this selectivity had existed, especially with senior staff.

In 1947, the post-Pacific War upheaval when the Occupation purged seniors thought to have had wartime responsibility, power reached the hands of younger men who then engineered Japan's postwar 'economic miracle'. This new crop of comparatively young men consolidated new hierarchies and held fast to their rank after their unexpected promotion. Until their retirement over thirty years later those who lived on held power and showed great reluctance to part with it. Despite exceptions and lip-service to youth being promoted over their seniors there are few indications in business, or politics, or the bureaucracy, of any weakening in the hierarchy of age.

Fraternities have their own grades amongst fraternities. The department head of a big company may outrank a director, or even a president of a smaller company. A professor in a small university may not have the status of a lecturer in a bigger university. A typist in an important fraternity takes pride in belonging and rates herself above a typist in a lesser company even though both may receive the same salary.

Installing a new fraternal leader is not always easy. He must be acceptable or the whole clique may disintegrate. Chie Nakane has stressed that the Japanese do not serve two masters. The stability of the hierarchy depends on a senior dominating at each level. Coalitions are difficult.

A man at a lower level within his organisation must channel his opinions and ideas up through his immediate superior. He should not communicate directly with those at higher levels. Communication upwards may, therefore, be slow and inefficient but downwards it can be speedy and effective. However, seniors rarely make decisions without seeking the agreement of the men who are the next step down the ladder. A man of low rank may exercise much greater influence than his status would seem to justify.

RANK VERSUS ROLE

In Western countries status and power are rarely divided. To the Japanese the custom of giving full authority to the man at the top is considered to be totalitarian. For ages Japan has maintained impressive figureheads with real power concealed behind 'black screens'. Over the last thousand years successive emperors have held the highest rank though exercising only formal power most of the time. Their approval, usually given automatically, confirmed important affairs of state. In their turn, the court officials and military commanders to whom the emperors had surrendered real power were themselves frequently little more than transmitters of authority. Members of their entourages played important roles in making the policies and in carrying them out in the name of their superiors. The system functioned at all levels. Nor is the significance of status without dictatorial power just a memory of the past. The rigid hierarchies survive because of the safety valve that the acual role of the individual need not, and often does not, correspond with his formal ranking.

The distinction between the titular heads who hold the final power and wielders of influence behind the screens is rarely stated explicitly, but at all times is understood and accepted implicitly within cliques. Deference must be given to those of higher rank and is expected from those of lower standing. A dominant person, who is not highest in the pecking order, must not openly challenge the authority of his seniors. A husband may be dominated by his wife, but she gives him formal deference. The ranking system is more than a façade and is always strictly maintained. As long as the façade is intact, power can be exerted from behind the screen.

Although power is with rank at every level, a dictatorial head is rarely as acceptable as the one who co-ordinates the team. Shigeru Okada, not long ago president of the large and old-established Mitsukoshi Department Store was a dictator until he was deposed by his fellow directors (not the shareholders) in 1982. There are numbers of other presidents who rule their companies despotically, but they are the exception, rather than the rule. 'One-man' companies are mainly small but include a handful of large ones. (The American magazine *Fortune*, in December 1984, said that some of Japan's most successful companies, it listed ten, were led by autocratic managers who made the decisions themselves.) Their presidents may make decisions without consultations, but in Japan the man at the top, although he holds the final power, rarely uses it without assurance that those below him will accept his decision. Presidents, directors and managers are symbols of unification, co-ordinators and communicators rather than men who make decisions by themselves. The Japanese say that when one is promoted to be a director one has reached 'the position of being directed'.

Team work, not the contribution of the individual, is the mainspring of Japan's social structure. If a capable junior's work becomes too obvious to outsiders and he takes personal credit for it, his high outside reputation causes hostility within the team. However, provided he co-operates with his associates and gives ritual subservience to the nominal head, the able and energetic man may in fact control the team in the leader's name. Dependence is not just the junior's reliance on his senior. By leaning on one another, the junior helps his senior to rise and is in turn elevated. The titular leader himself need not be brilliant. Unless he leaves things to the men below him they may resent not being given the opportunity to prove themselves. His success in the top position comes from his ability to leave work to his subordinates. At first glance decision making may be almost incomprehensible to the outsider.

DECISION-MAKING

The greatest difficulty in negotiating with Japanese organisations is to know with whom to deal. In other countries individuals have defined responsibilities and make decisions within the scope of their power. In Japan there is much less clarity. The president of an American company decides, the Japanese president approves.

Some commentators refer to decisions being made at the middle management level, not at the top. This avoids the issue. Middle managers screen what goes to the directors for decision and they implement the action after obtaining the agreement of the directors, but lower management must also consent. A consensus of all, not just the powerful middle level, is customary.

Seniors are constrained by the need to consult with and obtain the approval of their immediate subordinates who in their turn, before committing themselves, refer to their juniors and so on down the line. Lower down, however, approval may be almost automatic. The juniors' competition for promotion gives power to their seniors on whom they rely for selection.

Though token consultation at every rung of the ladder is a necessary part of the system, all participants are acutely aware that power is greater the higher the level. Even though the man who holds leadership at each level has to be cautious in exercising it, he holds the power to enforce. The status holder may be unlikely to make his decision until he is confident his followers approve it, but a hierarchical power structure exists and each leader at every level plays a positive role. In large organisations, when top management desires to implement a new policy an order or a hint may be given well down the line that a proposal be initiated in a standard form, circulated for approval in the lower ranks, and submitted upwards as quickly as possible.

The need for unanimity is formal to the extent that all groupings follow their acknowledged leader. He is the symbol and holder of power. He consults and if he finds opposition he will usually compromise with it in making his decision, but everyone knows he has power as well as the prestige of leadership. Juniors may conceal their real opinions and hesitate to suggest innovations and, to maintain harmony, they must suppress their personal opposition. To hold his position and the power that goes with it the senior may rely heavily and, in fact, follow the opinion of one or more of his subordinates, but the status holder's word when given is final.

Again the difference between Japanese and Western practice is one of degree, not of absolutes. While we Westerners are taught to stand separately as independent individuals we find that 'no man is an island'. We must work with others and settle our differences through communication with our fellows. To hold their positions, politicians and business leaders in the West may find it necessary to heed the advice of their peers and their juniors, and not to antagonise them, but they have a choice. They do not follow the overwhelming compulsion of a stratified system. The Western business executive has an option to move to another organisation if his decisions are not acceptable. There is little such mobility in Japan. Western leaders show confidence in themselves and may underestimate, or foolishly ignore, the power of others. Not so the Japanese. Dependency makes them constantly aware of the restrictions on their power.

The consensus needed by management is achieved after proposals have been scrutinised and modified and after many person-to-person informal discussions, interspersed with frequent meetings. Even managers are hesitant to put forward recommendations that may not be accepted or may cause embarrassment. The highly stylised culture has produced a fear of originality. Unique and creative ideas are often diluted into commonplace ones in the process. Dissension is suppressed. It is better to be silent than to disagree. Silence at a conference is a minus in the West. It is golden in Japan. Consensus decisions tend towards the lowest common denominator. The discussions are time consuming. Harmony is the overriding factor, to be achieved whatever the cost. Everyone in the team must confirm that he doesn't disagree, but each individual is only marginally responsible for the outcome. Everyone is competing for his own promotion up the ladder and this does not usually come to one who antagonises his peers or opposes his seniors.

Collective decision making cultivates a sense of unity, co-operative ties are strengthened. The participants' knowledge is deepened in matters in which they are not directly involved. It is useful training for young team-members and dissuades a despotic manager from going too far. Pressure for conformity produces self-restraint at the top as well as in the lower ranks. Management has to introduce change very carefuly to avoid commotion or violent reaction. Each individual and each group needs time to adjust to an emerging decision. (The method is likened to the time consuming root clipping undertaken before transplanting a tree.) By compromise and intuitive understandings, not by critical analysis, a generally acceptable decision emerges. Since all are concerned, a decision once made can be executed speedily. No further discussion is necessary. More than that. The process of wide participation in making decisions commits many persons to turning the project into a success. This strength lies behind large projects which have been discussed and agreed by government departments, banks and the whole company, or a group of companies, before the project is begun. The future of markets is always uncertain, but the Japanese businessman can embark on a new project with the confidence that even if things go wrong he has wide support to overcome problems.

Since many participants may not have been fully in favour of the first decision, an earlier absence of objection rather than the presence of agreement may lead to decisions being reversed if the situation changes. The clique, influenced by new external pressures, may suddenly swing from the enthusiasm of yesterday to support for its opposite today. Nevertheless, a policy, once set, is very difficult to challenge unless the situation changes. It is not easy for a minority to oppose the main-stream. The system has no room for conspicuous dissent. Acquiescence is essential to maintain consensus. 'The nail that sticks up must be hammered down.'

9 Obligations and the Law

OBLIGATIONS, POLITENESS, APOLOGY

Mutual dependence creates ever-present obligations which were and are imperatives. Some are clearly measurable and others firmly acknowledged but indeterminately defined and capable of flexible adjustment.

Obligations are a most active and ever-present ingredient in day-to-day affairs, as influential as the law in some decisions. The cash value of every present given or received is most carefully evaluated to keep a proper balance, but such exchanges, though frequent, are secondary. The greatest obligations arise from favours and assistance received. Their value may be hard to assess and cannot be measured in cash, but they are always remembered. Powerful but intangible obligations accumulate from birth, through marriage to death. Some 'debts' may never be fully settled no matter how much reciprocity is given and may be passed from one generation to the next. Although only in extreme circumstances should demand be made for settlement of obligations, they weigh heavily and must be repaid, voluntarily and with friendliness, as soon as possible.

The Japanese reluctance to be involved with outsiders comes partly from fear of creating obligations. On the other hand foreign strangers are guided to find their way in the street with an earnest enthusiasm rarely encountered in other countries and to a degree much greater than is customary between Japanese. Perhaps the sense of obligation is reduced with a total stranger which allows genuine thoughtfulness to be expressed and this mixes with a sense of obligation to guests, a desire that the Westerner will think well of Japan and, sometimes, a wish to practise a foreign language. Routine politeness is also present.

In the business world, if a Japanese company expects profit, a guest will be wined, dined and entertained on a scale more impressive than that experienced in any other country. The hosts feel that their hospitality will create an obligation which the guest must repay and that from the resulting business they will recoup the money spent on their guest's, and their own, entertainment. Vast amounts may be spent on a lucky visitor. He will be completely guarded so that he has neither time nor opportunity to see anything except that which his hospitable hosts want him to see. This entertainment, and confinement, is essentially a commercial exercise. It is not impossible that the visitor's firm may have profited more from its representative's trip if he had declined some of the hospitality and made a broader assessment of the market. On the other hand, some foreign visitors do not realise the obligations they have been placed under and may place orders with their hosts' competitors.

The visitor to Japan is impressed by the politeness which colours his encounters with everyone. For people living uncomfortably near to one another, formal politeness is a defence to prevent the disruption of social interrelationships. It also serves as a mask for true feelings. The cynic may point out that it is not to be confused with friendship. In the West we drop the formal Mr and use Christian names as we become friends. The Japanese affix 'san' as an honorific to one another's names (but not their own) in normal conversation. If I may add a note for the benefit of those who deal with Japanese, they rarely use first names in talking to persons other than their relatives or school classmates. In Japanese companies office workers rarely call each other by their first names. It has even been the custom to address fellow workers by the title of their rank rather than their surname. In brief, personal ('Christian') names are rarely spoken.

An aspect of politeness is the common expression of modesty, or humility. It is a part of Japanese etiquette to understate the capabilities of oneself or one's family and to deprecate the value of a gift. Where a foreigner would frankly and proudly admit, even boast, that his son was top of his class, or his wife a very good cook, many a Japanese with a bright son does not admit his pride. He may flatly deny his wife's talent in the kitchen.

When offered something, traditional good manners require of a Japanese that he should say, 'No, thank you'. The person offering is hard pressed to know whether the response is prompted by politeness or is genuinely meant. A housewife calling on an errand to a neighbour is always asked in for a cup of tea and always refuses. The lady of the house may repeat the invitation not once or twice but a dozen times and the visitor may refuse each request. When, eventually, she accepts or leaves the hostess may still wonder whether her visitor wanted to come in or was really in a hurry to be somewhere else. Convention cloaks real intentions. Nowadays

Japanese tend to be more forthcoming but misunderstandings are still frequent.

Japanese words which give thanks also include an apology. Japanese are moved by strong emotion when they are the recipients of goodwill. Foreigners do not have such over-sensitive reactions. We express our thanks briefly and that finishes the matter. Between Japanese the interweaving of apology with gratitude, and the almost magic affect of an apology, show characteristics which, if not unique, are certainly curious to a Westerner.

Doi has written:

> The Japanese are not content simply to show gratitude for a kind action but must apologize for the trouble which they imagine it has caused the other person . . . In other words, the matter is 'not ended' – something is still left over – because one has not done everything one should have done . . . . One [speaks] in the assumption that the kind deed has been a burden to the doer, and not, as Ruth Benedict suggests, from any immediate consciousness of the need to repay the kindness.

Instances of the efficacy of an apology are of everyday occurrence.

In December 1977, the Tokyo District Court under Presiding Judge Koji Tsuchikawa found Yosui Inoue, a popular singer and songwriter, guilty of buying and smoking marijuana and sentenced him to eight months in prison, but suspended the sentence because the singer had expressed penitence.

In March 1978 the Tokyo District Court sentenced Motoyoshi Kikuchi to nine years in prison for choking a foreign prostitute to death. The presiding judge, Takashi Sakamoto, said that the woman was working as hard as she could in a foreign land and the nature of her profession did not really matter. He based his lenient ruling on his belief that Kikuchi had shown signs of deep remorse for his crime.

Obligations, politeness, apology and the desire for harmony through compromise play significant roles in the functioning of the law.

LAWS

The customs, the social system and the old laws of Japan were based on duties, not rights. Although a hundred and more years ago some interests in land, forests and personal effects carried some entitledness along with some obligations, positive rights requiring other persons to acknowledge vested interests were not then definitely incorporated in the legal system. The traditional concept of social obligations did not carry the idea that legal rights were endowed in the individual nor a belief that the people had any right to criticise the law and those who made and enforced it. Neither legal writings nor everyday speech included any word that corresponded to rights as something due to a person and which he could claim.

When the West used force to open Japan's doors to outsiders, the invading nations found the Japanese judicial system incompatible with Western ideas of administering justice. They made treaties which prohibited the Japanese from prosecuting foreign nationals under Japanese law (and from determining customs duties on imports). The aliens lived in designated areas ruled by their own alien laws. To change the 'Unequal Treaties' Japan was required to institute laws acceptable to the West. In the last decades of the nineteenth century an entire new legal code was drafted and promulgated with language and philosophy following the European pattern. To achieve their Herculean task the legal draftsmen had to invent new Japanese words. In 1889 a new Constitution shifted the theoretical basis of Japanese law from duties to rights. A new, brilliant façade overlay the substance of traditional practice.

Although rights were granted, for the first time, in the Meiji Constitution, every right was qualified. Tradition dies hard, but the wide gap between the wording of the laws and their application in practice has narrowed over the years. The notion of rights has now become more than a balance to obligations. Hanami, in his *Labour Relations in Japan Today*, has said that,

> Japan has successfully applied a Western legal system without sacrificing traditional social values and culture . . . . To insist on legal rights is still regarded as tactless and indelicate . . . . Social relations must be maintained and they can be destroyed if either party stands on his rights.

A right, to be protected by law, should fit an objective standard which takes no account of situations. The Japanese are law abiding but do not accept a clear division between right and wrong, correct and incorrect, good and bad. They feel that in most disputes both parties are to blame.

> One evening I was driving home from the office along a narrow one-way street. A taxi came in the wrong direction. The driver of the

car in front of me pointed out his error. He stopped immediately and started backing. As I passed, the back of his car hit the side of mine. The accident was minor but the police had, of course, to be notified. After more than two hours intense discussion, they persuaded me to reach a compromise which they suggested and which made me equally responsible for the accident. The argument hinged on who had hit whom, a decisive yardstick in allocating blame for road accidents in Japan. I might have turned towards the centre of the narrow road too soon after passing the taxi whose driver was correctly hastening to back out of the road he should not have been in. And, of course, the taxi driver deserved sympathy because he was working for his living. That he should not have been where he was, the police did not consider relevant.

If a Japanese suffers injury or his property is taken by another, he feels that the offender is under obligation to recompense him for his injury or his loss. Expecting, or even claiming, the fulfillment of an obligation may not be different in essence from demanding the settlement of a right, but the approach tends towards negotiation rather than legal action.

It has been said that, 'The law is the last resort – its significance lies in not being invoked.' A majority of the Japanese people, when polled, have replied that laws are necessary but the courts are 'cold and distant'. They would consult their friends and superiors if they had legal problems. Conflicts are expected to be overcome by compromise and settled in accordance with human sentiment, by mediation. The Japan Arbitration Council has stated,

> In Japan conciliation is systematically incorporated into the judicial system . . . . Settlement by conciliation is allowed even if such settlement deviates from what the laws stipulate . . . . Conciliation includes compulsory features. For example, an interested party who is summoned to the conciliation proceedings is obliged to appear and if he fails to appear without any proper reason, he will be fined.

Many matters which are solved through legal processes in most other countries are handled in Japan without recourse to law. Even when the law is invoked the judge has wide latitude and need not follow decisions laid down by other judges in similar cases. Judgment is made after taking account of the intentions of the parties, past or existing inequities, and all the circumstances of the particular case. The judge's aim is an equitable compromise. Again to quote Hanami,

> Most contractual relationships are concluded and remain binding

solely on the basis of an amicable personal sense of friendship.' A direct expression of displeasure is considered a challenge to a friendly relationship. 'Rational conduct in the Western sense is ruled out in Japanese industrial relations.' It would lead to emotional disruption.

To settle disputes mutual trust and understanding must be established. Where the rift is large and neither side can lose face by making concessions a mutually respected third party is called in. He does not settle the dispute by reason or reference to any universal standards or by strict interpretation of the legal position. On purely emotional grounds he aims to restore friendly personal relations between the parties. Hanami recommends that this method could usefully be introduced into Western dispute procedures.

REGULATIONS

In Japan, separate from and contradictory to the vagueness of laws and obligations, all regulations must be followed to the letter. Sometimes I am intrigued by the subtle way in which the letter is obeyed while the intention of the regulation is neatly by-passed. Japanese ingenuity in this field needs to be seen to be appreciated and it is better not to give examples. It is in order, however, to give an example of the difficulty of interpreting some regulations.

The day that I wrote this paragraph I asked my Western bank manager if a transaction I proposed contravened any Japanese regulations. He checked with his Japanese staff and rang to say there was a regulation prohibiting the transaction. I proposed an alternative way of handling the matter. A few hours later he rang back to say that not only the second method was acceptable but also the first proposal did not contravene any regulation. He apologised, saying that he had obtained the new ruling when he had asked his staff why, if the second method was acceptable, the first was not. They had rechecked and found an alternative way of interpreting the regulations.

It is easy to quote cases where regulations and official instructions and documents are observed inflexibly.

'I need permission from my senior.' With these words, in February 1979, a Fukushima prefectural government guard odered firemen to stop using water while a raging fire destroyed a nearby three-storey furniture store. Later the guard explained, 'When I got a request from the fire station for water, I rushed outdoors and found firemen already taking water in the compound of our government office. I just thought I needed permission for such water use. I received permission from my senior over the telephone, but the firemen were already gone.'

The finality of the written official word was once made clear to a New Zealand newspaperman. A week before his permit to remain in Japan expired on 12 April 1953, he applied for its renewal and a few days later he received his amended card. (The facts of this incident I can vouch for though the dates are not exact.) Unfortunately he did not notice that the clerk who issued his new permit had inadvertently transposed the figures so that, according to the permit, he could stay in Japan from 12 April 1954 to 12 April 1953 instead of the other way round. Later in the year a policemen stopped him for driving beyond the speed limit. As his permit was valid for residence only till 12 April 1953, he was treated as an illegal immigrant and, though the clerical error was glaringly obvious, and the head of the local government department that had made the mistake was his friend, he had the utmost difficulty in avoiding immediate deportation. Even though it is known to be incorrect, an official record must be accepted at its face value.

In July 1980 the Osaka Handicapped Welfare Association had taken up the case of Chieko Yoshida a teacher of handicrafts who relied on a wheelchair as she had been a victim of infantile paralysis. She had insured herself thirteen years before with the Takatsuki City Accident Mutual Aid Plan. The policy covered accidents when riding automobiles, motorcycles, bicycles, or vehicles designated as public carriers such as trains. Ms Yoshida was hit and injured by a light van and her wheelchair overturned. The City organisation ruled that she could not claim under her insurance policy as wheelchairs were not named in it.

That laws remain open to case-by-case intepretation while regulations should be followed to the letter is really not the contradiction it at first appears. If the regulation of detailed contingencies were not rigorously enforced, the uncertain interpretation of broad all-embracing laws according to situations would lead to chaos in a culture that ignores universal principles. The two approaches to social living are but alternative parts of the same comprehensible whole.

CONTRACTS

In the small agricultural communities of the recent past, where everyone had the closest association with everyone else, written contracts were not necessary. Even in quite recent years some

Japanese have avoided contracts with a deep-seated notion that a contract presupposes that a man cannot be trusted without one. Formal, signed contracts, they feel, indicate distrust and a lack of harmony. In the West contracts have traditionally bridged the gap between peoples less intimately associated.

For many years I have tried with a conspicuous lack of success to explain to overseas principals that the agreements we negotiate and have our Japanese clients sign in the form of impressive contracts, drafted by lawyers in New York or London, do not carry the same weight in Japan as in America or Britain. In the West legal rules control the social order. A contract is less binding in Japanese eyes. To them an agreement should be valid only so long as the conditions under which it was made remain unchanged. The Japanese are governed, not by general principles, but by what is expedient.

The whole Japanese concept, of course, runs contrary to the basic principle of a contract. Some contracts, real estate transfers, patents and trademarks, are now accepted in Western terms but other Japanese contracts are often written ambiguously to allow for flexible interpretation. Their legal terms may create rights and obligations which are more apparent than real. By established custom, many include a clause which stipulates that the terms be reappraised if the situation changes substantially – a clause for 'consultation in good faith' or 'amicable consideration'. Even when such a clause has been omitted the practice is frequently endorsed, as if with the backing of common law. When disputes arise both sides expect to settle them by conference with mutual understanding and trust.

Whereas we aliens take the honouring of contracts most seriously, the Japanese still feel it is 'inhuman' to enforce them in changed circumstances. To the Japanese a contract is thought of as a memorandum of intent based on the situation at the time it was drawn up, the symbol of a relationship rather than an unchangeable legal document. In today's urbanised Japan contracts should perform the Western function and this is beginning to be the case, but old traditions die hard.

A classic breach of contract has been well publicised. In December 1974 Japanese sugar refiners signed a long-term contract to import from the Australian Sugar Board twenty per cent of Japan's raw sugar needs (about 600 000 tons) annually over five years ending in June 1980 at a fixed price of £229 per ton. The fixed price was about half the then world market price (about £400 per ton, a decline from a peak of £600 per ton), but the world sugar price fell dramatically to

£130 per ton within six months of the contract being signed. The Japan refiners found themselves committed to prices nearly double the new world level. Fulfilment of the contract had been guaranteed, at the time of signing, by an exchange of notes between the Australian and Japanese governments. Despite this, for about 16 months (from July 1976 to October 1977) the refiners requested a reduction in the fixed price. From July 1977 the refiners refused to take delivery and ship after ship lay idle incurring demurrage in Japanese ports. By November 1977 when the contract was eventually redrafted (the Japanese only achieved a 7 per cent price reduction with a compensating extension of the contract period) about 213 000 tons of sugar were waiting to be discharged.

Foreign Minister Ichiro Hatoyama summed up how Japanese deal with 'situations' as opposed to 'principles' when he declared on 13 September 1977: 'Japan would like to live up to its contracts. We are that kind of people. But this involves a question that if the contract is honoured, the [sugar refinery] companies will go out of business.' So much for a long-term 'contract' in Japan.

A Japanese contract tends to be so brief and general that a foreigner feels insecure. He prefers to know just where he stands. A Japanese feels the exact opposite. When terms are spelled out in explicit detail he feels insecure because he expects the situation will change before the contract is concluded.

In Japan relationships must be maintained. Harmony and conciliation are aimed at. Disputes should be settled out of court, perhaps using a go-between. Those who litigate are rejected by the system. Sticking up for your rights is trouble making. Personal relations are more real than abstract principles, or contractual agreements. It has been said that there are about 340 000 lawyers in the United States and only about 10 000 in Japan.

To indicate that my interpretation of the Japanese law is not just that of an experienced but perhaps prejudiced alien, I submit the view of a Japanese lawyer, Mariko Awaya, from the *Japan Times* of 3 March 1983:

Most people would be stunned if I said that no legal or contractual relationships exist in Japan. But this is a fact. Of course, Japan as a highly developed capitalist country, has a body of law and many contracts are concluded daily between individuals and business organisations. However, what is first established by 'contract' in Japan is a 'human relationship' between the parties concerned. What kind of rules are to be applied to problems that may arise between the two parties is decided not by the terms of a contract or laws, but by what kind of human relations have been established between them.

Foreigners who have signed a contract in Japan must have been puzzled by a passage at the end of the contract which said, 'When a dispute arises concerning this contract, the two parties will talk it over with sincerity'. (In Japan, this is called the 'sincerity clause'.) Even when they conclude a business deal worth billions of yen, Japanese do not set down detailed provisions in the contract regarding possible future problems and let the 'sincerity clause' perform this function. Western skepticism as to what an abstract idea like 'sincerity' can do to resolve disputes is irrelevant here. The clause is included on the premise that if good human relations exist between two parties, they will never fail to reach an agreement.

It is considered in Japan that the most important thing in resolving a problem is to settle it without destroying the human relationship between the parties concerned. Saving the face of both parties and maintaining amicable relations are more important than objective criteria or principles of reason in settling disputes . . . [The Japanese] society views the law as a hated entity which represents conflicts within the community rather than as something functioning to adjust conflicting interests within it . . . . Whatever disputes arise should be settled internally, and resorting to a means that affects 'outside' people goes against the rules of the community. Trying to settle a community dispute by resorting to outside rules – the law – is considered an act that destroys the illusion of community.

10 Religions, Mythology and Morality

RELIGIONS

Japanese religions have survived from time immemorial and play the same role in moulding Japanese thought and actions as has the deeply entrenched Christian ethic in the West. Japanese religions have little resemblance to Christianity.

'I turn to the Shinto priest in case of public festivals, while the Buddhist priest is my ministrant for funeral services. I regulate my conduct according to Confucian maxims and Christian morals. I care little for external forms, and doubt whether there are any essential differences, in the eyes of the Kami [Gods], between any of the religions of the civilized world.' So wrote a government spokesman, Professor Kunitake Kume, in 1910. His tolerant views broadly echo those of this countrymen, before and since.

For over a thousand years Japan has played host jointly to Shinto, Confucius and Buddha. Together the three intertwine in a system of ethics, morals and government that has shaped Japan through the centuries, though each religion has had its periods of dominance. Christianity was welcomed in the sixteenth century, flourished for two generations, suffered cruel persecution, was virtually exterminated, and permitted official re-entry little more than a hundred years ago.

Shinto

The ancient Japanese personified and worshipped all kinds of things – mountains, rivers, trees, stones, human beings. Shinto has no founder nor scriptures nor creed and has not developed clearly-defined philosophical doctrines other than an ideal of purity. Its appeal is aesthetic and intuitive. It is felt rather than understood. Though the rites imply certain moral standards, rituals more than ethical conduct have been of central importance in its observance. A Shintoist's belief in the oneness of humanity and divinity, concerns itself more with life in this world than in the next. An interest in tangible benefits is considered perfectly natural and stems from esteem for the gods that bestow and enhance life and worldly possessions.

In the beginnings of heaven and earth, we are told, there came into existence gods who created the islands of Japan and populated them. The early rulers claimed descent from Amaterasu, the Sun Goddess, and Shinto rituals held sway. Amaterasu's three holy relics – a mirror, a sword and a curved jewel – symbols of wisdom, courage and love, became and remain emblems of state. Government and ritual went hand in hand. Shinto prayers have been chanted unchanged in poetical liturgies from ancient times. The basic beliefs have been preserved down the ages as a cultural matrix on which imported foreign faiths have left their mark, but the doctrine of the gods underwent little modification even when the State used Shinto as an instrument of government between 1868 and 1945.

The leaders of the Meiji Restoration, as one of their first official acts after 1868, made 'State' Shinto a vehicle of power to unify the nation under their new government. Officially it was not designated as a 'religion' so that state support for Shinto did not have to be extended to 'foreign' religions – Buddhism and Christianity in particular. The government organised its teaching and indoctrinated the people with the concept of the family state with the emperor, a living god and direct descendant of Amaterasu, at its head. Under him was a family which included all citizens from high officials to poverty-stricken farmers and unemployed city labourers. State Shinto had total government support and, to justify the ultranationalism of the clan, took a form far removed from the original 'cult' Shinto.

State Shinto was suppressed by the Allied Occupation at the end of the Pacific War. Cult Shinto has remained, as informal as before. At present about 81 000 Shinto shrines (and 76 500 Buddhist temples) are being kept in repair.

Confucianism

Confucian philosophy came to Japan from China through Korea about AD 400 when Japan was being welded into a consolidated society under a single imperial house. The Chinese concept of the emperor as the Son of Heaven with a mandate to rule benevolently, through the exercise of virtue, the affairs of men and the world of nature was woven into native Shinto belief in many 'gods'.

Confucius had not indulged in metaphysical pondering or

devotional ecstasy, but had concerned himself with the family unit as the base of the social structure and filial piety as the highest virtue, with submission to parents and political leaders as parts of the foundation. Confucianism, intellectual and rational, became from time to time the official orthodoxy of the State. It laid great stress on prescribed forms of conduct that gave cohesion and stability to the social order.

Up to 1867 the Tokugawa government had incorporated Confucianism in its administrative theory and practice and 'the only religions to which the government paid serious attention' (this quotation comes from a government-sponsored publication in 1972) 'were Buddhism, to which it gave a place of honor; Shinto which it largely ignored; and Christianity which it proscribed'.

Edwin Reischauer has written that, although few Japanese think of themselves as being Confucianists, almost all are, even today.

Buddhism

Buddhism as found in Japan has been adapted and modified to meet local tastes. Introduced to Japan early in the sixth century AD from India by way of China and Korea, it was not accepted without opposition, but Shinto's lack of a formal doctrine reduced the conflict. Buddhist priests adjusted their teachings to include Shinto gods as reincarnations of Buddhist deities. Both beliefs lived side by side.

Buddha was a foreign god from a distant country, but the imported statues and carvings were admired for their beauty. Buddhist temples, sometimes combined with Shinto shrines, were constructed, and in them Buddhist priests chanted sutras and performed Buddhist rites for the enlightenment of the Shinto gods. The Japanese introduced magical beliefs into their interpretation of Buddhism, and the holding of services for the dead became of central, practical significance as compared with the original teachings of the Buddha which made their main purpose the attainment of enlightenment. Buddhist enlightenment, in Japan, became 'understanding things within the phenomenal world', and Nichiren, founder of a still influential Buddhist sect, laid down: 'Action according to things. Not action according to principles.'

Buddhist philosophers have searched for the true self and to realise it through a unique experience. All Zen sects believe that transmission of enlightenment does not depend on teaching, but that direct communication goes straight to the heart without written words. Putting knotty philosophical problems in place of formalistic rituals, they try to bring Buddhism into daily life. While Zen Buddhism was very much the religion of the warriors, the Nichiren, Amidist and Shingon Buddhist sects were powerful influences on Japanese life through the centuries and Nichiren, through its more recent offspring, in particular Soka Gakkai and Rissho Koseikai is very much a living force today.

New Religions

Based on the teachings of Buddhism and the religious experiences or personalities of their founders, these have been frequent phenomena in Japan. Many groups have faded out of existence soon after their birth. Others, including Tenri, Kyuseikyo, Soka Gakkai, and Rissho Koseikai, have grown at an explosive pace to gigantic dimensions. Their millions of followers and their great activity make it impossible to overlook those sects which still have the support of huge bodies of adherents.

The impulse to accept a new faith has come from lonely, displaced people. Rapid industrialisation and the surge to cities and towns have separated millions from the traditional worship they had followed in their native villages. The new religions concern themselves very much with this world. New movements promise to rescue people from adversity by essentially magical techniques which restore health to the sick and happiness to victims of misfortune.

Christianity

Christianity, in the person of Francis Xavier, a Portuguese Jesuit priest, came to Japan first in 1549. For about fifty years the missionaries, particularly in the southern island of Kyushu, exercised an influence vastly exceeding their numbers which were rarely more than a hundred including Japanese. They converted as many as 300 000 persons out of a total population of between 15 and 20 millions.

The feeling that Christianity is a 'foreign religion' is still strong among the Japanese people. This foreignness has been an advantage to the missionaries at some times and a grave handicap at others.

In three periods Christianity made rapid progress: the first arrival of the Jesuits, coinciding with the closing years of centuries of civil war; the opening of Japan to Western influences of all sorts from 1868; and the post-Pacific War Occupation of the country by the Allied armies from 1945 to 1952. At these times the very foreignness of Christianity was its greatest asset. People turned to it because it represented something new.

In the sixteenth and nineteenth centuries and during the Occupation, the Japanese tradition of loyalty to superiors was transposed to loyalty to a transcendent God. This concept was frowned upon by the government, especially in the first case when it was suspected that Christianity might be a foreign political lever associated with the danger of military invasion. In the later Meiji era Christianity was also looked upon as subversive because it taught that all men were equal and secular authorities were not absolute. This struck at the Japanese value system and jeopardised total loyalty to the Emperor.

The growth of Christianity in Japan since 1945 has been far from remarkable. Whereas many millions of people have joined the new indigenous religions which have blossomed since the war, Christians still number substantially under one million, less than one per cent of the population. Other imported faiths, Buddhism and Confucianism, were adapted without conflict of values.

Tolerant acceptance of many faiths and indifference to dogma, coupled with an absence of conspicuous outward manifestations of regular religious worship such as Sunday, or weekly, services at the multitude of temples and shrines, have led many Western followers of the strict Christian faith to dub the Japanese people as irreligious though few dispute their having a 'sense of religion'.

Some Christian missionaries say that the Japanese wear religion lightly, or that the Japanese consciousness is so based on family or communal dependence that it cannot accept a religion of individual choice and commitment. In Japanese eyes, the Christian missionaries have a 'conversion orientation' which inhibits their ability to understand other religions. As examples of Japanese religious rituals, they point to Shinto agricultural rites, children's ceremonies, rituals to drive away disease and ill-fortune, and to great throngs of worshippers at shrine festivals. In the home, many household Shinto shrines and Buddhist altars receive daily offerings. Ancestors are venerated in accordance with Buddhist rites, family graves are maintained, priests are asked to chant sutras on the occasion of funerals and on designated days related to deaths, while mortuary tablets of departed family member are kept on household Buddhist altar shelves. Marriage is celebrated nowadays with Shinto or Christian ceremony. (Marriage in a Christian church does not require that either bride or groom be Christian.)

It has been pronounced, and few would disagree, that tangibility is an essential part of the Japanese approach to religion. The abstract concepts of Western philosophies, ideologies and religions are still quite strange to most Japanese who preoccupy themselves with an overwhelming need to preserve human relations amidst the worldly concrete realities of living together.

Though imported religions have been assimilated and adapted for fourteen hundred years, no foreign religion has been forced on Japan by military conquerors. Imported religions have passed through thick filters and only those parts acceptable to the materialism of the deeply entrenched human relations communal system have been incorporated.

The Cultural Affairs Agency records ninety million Shintoists and eighty-eight million Buddhists and an estimated fourteen million persons who follow other religions. This gives a total of one hundred and ninety-two million believers. The whole population of Japan is about one hundred and twenty million! The nominal membership of faiths is obviously misleading. Despite or perhaps because of their plurality of religious affiliation, few Japanese take an active part in frequent religious observances. Japanese religions conform with a competitive-communistic economic structure.

MYTHOLOGY AND SUPERSTITION

If Japan has an abstract ideology, where better to find it expressed than in a book published by a semi-government department in time of war. Let us turn again to Hasegawa in 1940.

> Since most countries of the world do not represent the ethnic stock as it was when that mythology took shape, it is almost impossible to judge of the national character of any country on the strength of its mythology alone. Such is not the case, however, with the Japanese nation ... as it is a comparatively pure stock free from the racial confusion caused by immigration and conquest, Japanese mythology may safely be taken as a faithful mirror of the national character ...
>
> The Japanese character is proof against disintegration originat-

ing in the development of religion and learning ... because it is permeated by an element of concreteness rather than of abstraction, of practicality rather than theoretic speculation .... Fundamental instincts found ethical and philosophical expression in ... a system of learning which might be called 'primitive Confucianism' ... but the Japanese mental soil was not favorable to a prosperous growth of a metaphysical form of Confucianism, the practical side alone influencing, though powerfully, the ethics of feudal Japan .... The Japanese psychology was not hospitable to other branches of Chinese learning which were brought over to Japan together with Confucianism .... That the Japanese have had no metaphysics and philosophy of their own is true in the sense that they possessed no such schools in systematised form. Japanese metaphysics and philosophy have been embodied in the life of the people itself ....

Japanese soil has never been favorable to those negative and nihilist systems of metaphysics and philosophy which sprang up from time to time in civilized countries of antiquity as if by the exigencies of Fate. Though Indian philosophy was zealously studied by the ancient Buddhists in Japan, their mastery of Buddhistic doctrine, priests as they were, consisted in handling the subject as a constructive instrument of learning in the same way as they regarded Confucianism and Taoism .... Abstract ideas divorced from life the Japanese considered as lacking significance even from the academic point of view. They even went so far as to regard such a separation as a violation of morality.

To bring Hasegawa up to date, let us refer to Roy Andrew Miller who, in 1978, has written intriguingly and controversially of the Japanese language itself being a modern myth. Miller's opinion is not accepted by all scholars but it deserves to be aired.

The Japanese approach their language within a mystical framework supported by a mythical foundation of beliefs about its structure and operation .... One of the principal functions of a myth is to provide a focus for a social group, a common point about which that group may center its life and work. This focus is immune to the otherwise normal concerns of logic, reason, and common sense, and for that reason it is all the more important and durable. This is the role that the modern myth of the Japanese language in Japan plays so superbly .... A hundred voices are raised in

Japan every day attesting to the durability of the myth and perpetuating its mystical phenomenology, or trappings, but one looks almost in vain in the literature for a single voice arguing against the myth .... The myth is modern in the sense that it is a vigorous component of the modern scene; it is modern in the sense that it is an integral part of the thinking and intellectual equipment of modern Jápanese life and culture; but it is not modern in the sense that it is something manufactured in recent times or produced in our day for some particular goal or end. The essential ingredients of the myth have been available within Japanese literary culture since the time of the Man'yoshu anthology .... A large number of essential concepts, ideas, standards, and patterns of behavior have been perpetuated more or less unchanged across the dimension of time, despite the major alterations in more visible aspects of Japanese life.

An example of the attitude described by Miller is a statement by Akira Tsujimura, Professor of Social Psychology, Tokyo University, who says,

If the foreigners are to understand Japanese culture they would never do it by their phonetic Western language systems. I feel that the Japanese people and the Japanese language are the only ones that can combine East and West .... The Japanese culture can only be truly understood when the state of 'selflessness' is understood.

The Japanese nourish what in Western eyes are myths and superstitions and have not developed abstract intellectual concepts or religions with the universal values which have thrived elsewhere. They have always conceived of the supernatural at the human level, their earliest gods sharing earthly dwellings and a life of this world. Those who do not accept such beliefs or hold opposing ones are likely to label them as outright superstitions, but has it not been said that superstition is the other man's religion? In Japan outward manifestations of such 'superstitions' are still to be seen on every hand.

In the early months of each year students and their parents stream to temples and shrines to offer prayers and gifts for examination success. At the Kameido Shrine in eastern Tokyo they buy paper oracles costing 30 yen to tie to trees around the shrine, or more expensive 1000 yen charms to take away. If they pay a priest 3000 yen he will read their names – usually ten at a time – clap and invoke the gods to help them with their examinations. For 10 000 yen a priest will offer a prayer daily for one year on behalf of a student.

Other students buy good-luck souvenirs in unexpected places. Ricky, a gorilla at Ritsurin Park Zoo in Takamatsu, has been flooded with letters of thanks and presents of fruit and cash from successful examination candidates all over the country. The superstition stems from Ricky's habit of flinging his dung against the netting of his cage. Examination candidates regard this as a good luck omen because 'un' meaning dung sounds similar to the word for good-luck. The zoo authorities have seen an opportunity and sell good luck charms with pictures of the gorilla sitting on his dung.

These student beliefs conflict with a 1979 official survey which reported that seven out of ten young Japanese did not profess to any religion. Or do they?

Every month huge crowds gather at the Zeniarai Benten Shrine in Kamakura on the days of the snake to wash their money, even their bank-notes, sometimes protected in vinyl bags. Housewives, students and businessmen, some from hundreds of miles away, believe or hope that the Shrine god, Uga Fuku-no-kami, will see to it that if they spend the money promptly it will return two-fold in one day.

Thousands of Buddhist temples and Shinto shrines regularly cater to the desires of the populace. Ladies who want to be beautiful flock to the Sentoji Temple or the Mikunigozen Shrine in Kyoto. To pray that their husbands' tempers be moderated they turn to Mushifuujino-Anayawata, and to cure their children who misbehave to Kakanzan Daisoji, both in Tokyo. The Kanshadensha of Yawata Shrine in Kyoto accepts prayers for forgiveness for lies told during the previous twelve months. The Yasui Konpiragu helps those who want to stop smoking, drinking or gambling.

1966 was the year of the Fire Horse, an event that occurs once every sixty years in the Zodiac cycle (a combination of twelve animals and five elements). The remarkably small number of registrations of the births of girl-children in 1966 and the extremely large number in 1967 reflects the popular belief that girls born in the year of the Fire Horse are fierce and not to be married. It is generally believed that parents put off registrations until the following year in order to protect their offspring from later handicap.

MORALITY

We Westerners approach day-to-day life conditioned to universal abstract concepts of 'good' and 'evil', embracing all situations. Our values change from generation to generation and vary from person to person, but Westerners have broad standards against which to measure what we believe is right and what is wrong.

To the Japanese morality interweaves with human relations. They

do not accept abstractions as a guide to what is 'good' or 'evil'.
Universal standards are considered meaningless and even objection-
able. Most things are permissible when the occasion is appropriate.
The 'flesh' is not evil. They accept anything as natural as sex as
neither good nor bad. Enjoyment of the pleasures of the body has
never been correlated with sin. The 'soul' and the 'body' are not in
contention. The Japanese are not Puritans. They do not condemn
the pleasures of the body provided they do not intrude on the
'serious' affairs of life such as subjugation to the community and the
performance of allotted tasks. To carry out boring, routine work
with persistence and sincerity is a good thing in itself. Excesses are
less acceptable but even here it is a matter of the situation, not the
thing itself. Dual standards are expected when dealing with insiders
(members of cliques) or outsiders. Goodness and badness are relative
to human interrelationships and to the circumstances with all
their complexities. The aim is harmony through self-control and
compromise.

It is not that the Japanese see no distinction between good and
bad. Prince Shotoku's sixth-century constitution, Article VI said,
'Punish the vicious and reward the virtuous. This is the excellent
rule of antiquity. Do not, therefore, let the good deeds of any person
go concealed, nor the bad deeds of any go uncorrected, when you
see them. Flatterers and deceivers are like the fatal missile which
will overthrow the state, or the sharp sword which will destroy the
people.' Later, the warriors' code laid down that warriors should do
nothing mean or despicable, even at the cost of their lives.

Some Japanese Buddhist priests are celibate. Many followers
are vegetarians, some are teetotallers and some practise religious
austerities, but the Buddhist belief that personal desire is evil has
not been widely accepted by the Japanese. Human nature, they
believe, is naturally good. Sincerity overcomes our impurities. The
purity that comes from self-control leads to serenity, the Buddhist
ideal of the detached self, but few Japanese see virtue in fighting
evil. Materialistic desires, as such, may also be enjoyed. Japanese
do not think of pleasure as being in any way evil, but to give up a
pleasure shows strength of will which is a virtue and admirable.

Sincerity, the greatest virtue, does not carry its Western meaning.
To the Japanese it incorporates behaviour that does not cause
offence to anyone and, in theory at least, the rejection of self-
seeking. Japanese feel that an expression of sincere intentions is
enough and not subject to proof – circumstances may abort action.

While eminently this-worldly and materialistic the Japanese must conform to group pressures and impress their intimates with their sincerity. I have been struck by the scrupulous honesty of the individual Japanese and, not to put too fine a point on it, the ruthless self-interest of large, world-famous, Japanese trading companies who, often exploited in the past by the sharp practices of foreign carpet-baggers, have learned from them.

Japanese cynics say that tears of apology and the deepness of the bow may just be play-acting and means of deception but remorse is taken as a step towards the accused's rehabilitation. 'Purity' of motives can excuse and gain wide public support for apparently anti-social acts, as witness the acceptance by the Japanese people of prolonged, violent riots by a section of the public against the government while the Narita airport at Tokyo was under construction and even long after it had opened.

It has been said that shame dominates Japanese behaviour while Westerners give priority to feelings of guilt. Ruth Benedict wrote about Japan thirty years ago

> True shame cultures rely on external sanctions for good behaviour, not, as true guilt cultures do, on an internalized conviction of sin. Shame is a reaction to other people's criticism. A man is shamed either by being openly ridiculed and rejected or by fantasying to himself that he has been made ridiculous. In either case it is a potent sanction. But it requires an audience or at least a man's fantasy of an audience. Guilt does not. In a nation where honor means living up to one's own picture of oneself, a man may suffer from guilt though no man knows of his misdeed and a man's feeling of guilt may actually be relieved by confessing his sin.

The two emotions are closely associated and their effects similar. An assumption that shame and guilt are unrelated is extreme. Status conscious Japanese, dependent on the reaction of their fraternity members, are undoubtedly sensitive to shame, but this does not mean that they are immune from feelings of guilt or that Westerners are not influenced by shame if their conduct is socially disapproved. Although the Japanese fraternity-oriented mixture weighs heavily on the side of shame and individualistic Westerners swing to the side of guilt, the difference should not be exaggerated.

The Japanese judge each situation on its merits through eyes which take account of the human relations involved and the facts as they appear to each beholder. Loyalty to their clique and their superiors is the aim. Where principles are not treated as important and where there is no ideology, this boils down in practice to the ethics of expediency and utility. It has been said that the basic religion of twentieth-century Japanese is faith in Japan.

11 Communication

LANGUAGE

To link the ancient communal system with today we can see how it has survived, undisturbed by foreign conquerors, through the retention of old customs, religions and myths passed on by childhood training but we must not neglect the power of an unusual language.

The Japanese hesitate to employ language explicitly to convey definite thoughts or intentions. Rather than reveal their opinions at all positively they proceed cautiously. The habit of vagueness has strong historical justification. Age-old dependence on communal living based on rice farming, with its regular routines carried out by the same people year after year, reduced the need for speech. In addition, constant surveillance made it unwise and dangerous to express opposition to the rule of the central government or local lords.

As early as AD 1597 a foreign observer, Francisco Carletti, noted that, 'Very little escapes the minute vigilance exercised by the authorities of the cities'. Even villagers had good reason to fear the widespread secret police network. Informers infiltrated all levels of society. Had you lived in those days and, during a convivial evening, a fellow villager suggested anti-government action to combat the oppressive taxation, you would have been in a dilemma. You would not have been sure whether he had been ordered to make the treasonable statements to you and that if you did not report his words you would be arrested.

Less than fifty years ago 'dangerous thoughts' led to jail and even death. The Japanese no longer carry the burden that existed during the youth of men who now guide their destinies, but many have yet to learn that the absence of meaningful dialogue can be a serious hindrance in a modern, complicated society which requires communication with 'outsiders'.

The difficulty of mastering the language, which embalms much from the past, plays a role in concealing the Japanese culture from aliens. It is not just that the Japanese language is itself unique, all languages are, but unless the nuances are comprehended, grammar and vocabulary are insufficient.

The hurdle of the spoken and written word is not the only barrier to understanding. To a Japanese empty space and silence are neither nothingness nor static. They can be as significant as things themselves. A Westerner flounders until he grasps the importance to the Japanese of nothing having the same qualities as something. To them, what is not said can be as important as what is said. Actions are based on assumptions, often wrong, of what the other person intends or wants.

When two Japanese businessmen discuss a proposition they return to their respective desks and each thinks about what the other said and what he didn't say. Each then makes his assessment of the other's real intentions. If one man has not said something because it had not occurred to him, he may have confused his opposite number immeasurably.

NON-VERBAL COMMUNICATION

Verbal transmission is supplemented by intuitive comprehension of what is not said. Communication is partly visual. The Japanese say, 'The eyes are more expressive than the mouth. The wise do not talk. The talkative are not wise.' They add that they do not trust words and their words are not meant to be trusted. To them sensitivity to what is in a person's mind should make speech superfluous; the use of words evidences a lack of understanding; sympathy submerges thoughtless words; verbal skill is for those at arm's length; silence is a sign of honesty and trustworthiness. To merge intimately with others, to communicate feelings that have to be understood intuitively is, they feel, more effective than verbal exchanges. The variety of these expressions indicates the strength of communal feelings and the obstacles to individualism.

Followers of Zen reject dependence on words, verbal or written, for the transmission of Buddhist enlightenment. It has been said that foreigners listen only to the words between pauses while the Japanese listen to the pauses between words. To them silence can be pregnant. A break between words may convey a richer meaning than the words themselves. To prevent misunderstandings the single most important lesson a Westerner must learn is the necessity of listening.

To communicate without speech is a talent not unknown or uncommon in the West. On the contrary, even though we may not be aware of it, we Westerners use silent language every day. Our attitudes are constantly conveyed without words by gestures, smiles, frowns, silence and innuendo. Westerners who live closely together frequently reach understanding without speech, but the non-verbal plays a much larger part in the lives of the Japanese.

Needless to add, non-verbal communication relies on physical proximity and highly developed mutual understanding. The habit reflects a society subdivided into small clusters of people who live closely and know one another intimately. While effective for small groups, it fails between casual Japanese acquaintances within industrialised, urban Japan and it seriously impedes international understanding.

SPEAKING AND WRITING

The high hurdle of language competence can be cleared without, of itself, enabling the Westerner to communicate effectively with Japanese. Concentration on vocabulary and grammar may hobble an appreciation of vague subtleties as much as non-verbal comprehension. It is not unusual for one of my Japanese staff, when reporting a business conversation with someone in another company, to say, 'I don't think what he said is correct. There was a difference in his expression', or, 'I think I detected a change in his voice when he said it.' In writing as well as in speech, what is not said can be more important than what is said. Obscure language plays a significant role in aborting communication and making Japan probably the most misunderstood country in the world. Communication is in fine shades. So many words and phrases have more than one meaning. Ask three Japanese to translate some letters into English and three quite different interpretations may be given. Even in business correspondence, my Japanese staff often say they do not understand important parts of letters we have received in Japanese. The Japanese respect a person who can converse with two persons with opposing views and part with both thinking he supports them. Understanding depends on intuition founded on an underlying feeling for the motivations of persons and the ways they express themselves. It is 'not what you say but the way that you say it'.

The language mirrors the relationship and feelings between the speakers, often in abbreviated form without a full statement of the subject and object, omitting as superfluous matters which are thought to need no explanation to people who know each other and the environment. The subject comes at the start of the sentence and there may be many confusing clauses between it and the verb which often comes at the end and always well after the subject. The words that express the fundamental nature of each sentence come at the end. In conversation, to avoid direct statement, the sentence may not even be completed.

A wealth of personal pronouns and strict canons of respect language show hierarchical evaluations and the relationships between the people involved. On the other hand, the language is weak in status-neutral vocabulary. Although conversation as equals is not uncommon, the Japanese language embodies an assumption that each individual is either superior or inferior. Children and women have languages different from men. The choice of words depends on who is addressed – a senior or a junior, a man or a woman, a colleague, a student. Rank dictates what each person is expected to say. Real opinions may only be expressed in private, informal circumstances between two parties who know one another well.

Edwin Reischauer has written that the common complaint that the Japanese language is too lacking in clarity or logic to fit modern technological or scientific needs is balderdash and he points out that all languages have infinite capacities for ambiguities and obscurities. Lest this give the impression that translation and interpretation between Japanese and foreign languages is not extremely difficult, Reischauer adds that it is probably easier to be ambiguous and vague in Japanese than in Western languages and that the Japanese usually prefer to avoid logical argument and clear statements. Although the Japanese language itself may not be vague it is frequently used in a vague way. Miller, who has been quoted on myths, has also written:

> Scholarly prose is so dense that in many cases even specialists in the field in question are hard put to answer direct inquiries about just what the text is trying to say about what. It is writing that, since it does not communicate to the reader anything at all about what the author is trying to say, violates the most elementary and functional definition of language as a medium of social interrelationship. Yet, writing of this variety is not only prized by many Japanese scholars and intellectuals but the techniques for its generation are carefully cultivated.

When the Emperor went on the air in 1945 and announced the termination of the war, he used literary language. Some listeners are said to have mistakenly thought that he had said a decisive battle would begin on the Japanese mainland.

To say 'no' bluntly is thought to be impolite and to ignore the feelings of the other party. Ideas are conveyed indirectly. 'I will think about your proposal,' often means a refusal. Masaaki Imai has written that,

> In Japan one is not supposed to say 'no'. It is rude, impolite, uncivilized, demoralizing, and hurts the feeling of the other party. Saying 'no' is a capital sin in Japan. One has to be tactful and diplomatic enough to resort to such art as euphemism and body-language in order to convey his negative message. Foreign businessmen who are unable to interpret these unique Japanese behaviours at the conference tables have to undergo a bitter and costly experience in terms of an unfulfilled order, disappointment, and the costly executive time wasted. In my English book, '*Never Take Yes for an Answer*,' I wrote that 'yes' does not always mean yes in Japan and that there are some sixteen ways to avoid saying no and that to call a spade a spade is not in the Japanese tradition. The first and perhaps most typical way of saying no is to say yes first, followed immediately by an explanation which may last half and hour and which, in effect, means no. One has to be very attentive since the tone of the response is always affirmative throughout the conversation. Don't be misled by the affirmative tone. Concentrate only on the contents and find out if you can get a firm commitment for the next step. The second way of saying no is to be vague, ambiguous, and evasive in one's reactions so that the other party becomes confused and lost to the extent that he cannot even remember what the issue was. By sending out contradicting signals, the Japanese businessman hopes that the other party will get the hint and take the initiative of calling off the talk itself. The third way is not to answer the question directly and simply leave the matter unattended. The postponement of a decision on a pending issue is tantamount to saying no, a tactic often employed by government officials. Other ways include changing the subject abruptly, criticizing the other party, or suddenly assuming a highly apologetic tone . . . . When a foreign visitor is not certain whether he is getting a negative signal or not, he may be advised to ask simple negative questions, such as 'Do you think we had better call off the negotiation?' and 'Do you think our next meeting is not necessary?' That might save the Japanese businessman the embarrassment of having to say no.

To convey something of the 'feel' of non-verbal and vague communication *haragei*, a word with no clear English equivalent, deserves brief mention. Michihiro Matsumoto, in 1978, popularised the concept in Tokyo's English language press. He said the best dictionary definition is that *haragei* 'deals with things or situations through the belly (Japanese plunge their swords into their stomachs, not their hearts) and experience beyond formalities and logic'. *Haragei* is effective emotionally or instinctively without the use of words or by employing vague inconclusive words. It is, therefore, an extension of normal Japanese conversation which is rarely definitely positive or negative and is a 'combination of mind and gut'. I have discussed *haragei* with Matsumoto and, no doubt in support of its basic practice, we talked in circles and finished where we started.

Haragei is, by definition, the complete opposite of debate. It has been described as the art of tight-rope walking in everyday affairs and as 'the Japanese art of deception'. To mystify a little further, Matsumoto lists some 'don'ts' at the heart of *haragei* (he says he can expand the list from 15 to 145):

1. Don't tell the truth, but don't tell lies.
2. Don't make friends, but maintain 'hostile friendship' (friends may become enemies).
3. Don't debate.
4. Don't define yourself.
5. Don't say 'no'.
6. Don't justify yourself.
7. Don't attract attention to yourself.
8. Don't be direct.
9. Don't ask why.
10. Don't explain why.
11. Don't be specific.
12. Don't show emotions.
13. Don't seek identity.
14. Don't be predictable.
15. Don't be independent.

Haragei, Matsumoto says, is the art of saying 'no' without saying 'no' and saying 'yes' without saying 'yes' and he also lists ways to avoid saying 'no'.

1. Avoid answering.
2. Be extremely polite.
3. Explain the situation, don't give reasons.
4. Inflate the other person's ego while deflating yours.
5. Deliberately avoid the central issue.
6. Use vague language.
7. Make your argument abstract and metaphysical.
8. Pity yourself.
9. Generalise from the particular.
10. Keep the other person guessing.

11. Say 'yes, but . . .'
12. Make a sacrificial lamb of somebody.
13. Arrange for a third party to say 'no' for you.

The Japanese language is far from static. Almost daily, new foreign words are adopted in writing and conversation. Their number has grown unbelievably. A recent dictionary lists 25 000 foreign words. While the military ruled prewar Japan the incorporation of foreign words into the language was discouraged. The recent adoption of so many has been quoted as evidence that the Japanese are becoming Westernised and are no longer nationalistic. This is a superficial judgment. The newly accepted words are customarily deformed to fit their new home and are sometimes used to convey concepts widely varying from their Western meanings. Their proliferation does not necessarily bridge the communication gap but they illustrate Japan's ability to assimilate foreign ideas and incorporate them as their own with no feeling that this in any way diminishes Japanese stature.

With its two alphabets (three if we include Japanese words written in Romaji – our alien alphabet – which creep in frequently) plus at least two thousand ideographs which retain the essential appearance and some of the meaning of their Chinese originals, the written Japanese language presents special problems. In the West we first learn an alphabet and from this we learn to make, pronounce and write words. The intricate Japanese method of writing, like the Chinese and in opposition to the European, is essentially visual, not phonetic. Instead of learning to combine letters to form words, the Japanese child must copy and reproduce words to be comprehended as a whole in their own right. The years of memorisation required to acquire the written language retards mental agility. On the other hand, this picture writing has nurtured a native artistry. Every child learns to draw as he learns to write.

Whatever the virtues of the Japanese language, it has some very great defects in the day-to-day management of an office. Because of its complexities it does not lend itself to dictation. The Japanese executive customarily writes a letter or memorandum in longhand or conveys the outline of what he wishes to say to a secretary who prepares a draft in longhand for his correction or approval. The typing of letters is a slow process. Japanese typewriters have two trays containing 3300 characters. The one selected must be located, picked up by a claw-like attachment and impressed through an inked ribbon. Because typing is so slow, most companies rely on handwriting and employ teams of scribes, usually male, as a business letter in feminine handwriting may be considered unsatisfactory. Word processors and memory machines solve many difficulties. They are being used more and more widely, but they are still expensive. Storage in computers of information written in Japanese is also time consuming and costly. Photocopying machines are very useful in offices throughout the world. In Japan they are indispensable.

Without assessing the balance of advantages and disadvantages it should be recorded that the Chinese have begun to phase ideographs out of their written language. The Japanese have not been prepared to make such a decision. Resistance to this basic change may be attributed to a strong preference for the traditional and the absence of Western rationality. The Japanese are extremely practical but this could be an example that, by Western standards, they are not rational.

Against the basic social framework of cliques, dependence, rationality, traditions and communication we can look more closely at the ways in which Japanese society operates through the place of women and their power in supervising childhood training.

12 Women

MATRIARCHY?

The late Daisetsu Suzuki, world-known for his interpretation of Zen Buddhism, has written that the father is at the root of Westerners' thinking and feeling, but the mother is deep-seated in the essence of the Oriental nature. Though not everyone agrees with his verdict, Kiyoaki Murata, then editor of the *Japan Times*, wrote in 1980 that, 'Japan has been, still is, and is even more so today than before, a matriarchal society.' Should 'matriarchy' imply descent through the female line, the term 'mother obsession' may better describe the powerful maternal influence in Japan's social system. Mother obsession is a common theme in Japanese literature, ancient and modern.

The West has long believed that Japanese women are relegated to virtual slavery and much has been written about the need to liberate them. There is glaring and indisputable evidence that women who work are discriminated against, but the picture of male domination must be kept in perspective by taking into account the position of women in the home. The trappings of power decorate the husband, but history and current experience show how careful one must be in judging anything in Japan from superficial appearance. There is duality of rank and role, of power behind the 'black screen'.

The mythological founder of Japan was a woman, Amaterasu, the Sun Goddess. For centuries descent was matriarchal. From the end of the sixth century until the late eighth century half of the rulers of Japan were women – eight out of sixteen sovereigns, although two reigned twice. Between the tenth and thirteenth centuries well-educated women wrote elegant poems and diaries and played prominent parts in the culture of the court. Before AD 1600 there was little difference in the speech of men and women. Today the intimacy and dominance of the mother, established and encouraged during children's formative years, comes through into adult life.

The Japanese wife is solely responsible for bringing up the children and her influence inside the home is acknowledged. What is less well known is that, though she might have walked at a respectful distance behind her husband when he strolled abroad, and she still accepts a submissive role in public, the majority of wives in this day and age receive their husbands' full wages every pay-day. The wife gives her husband pocket-money for his fares, his lunch, his cigarettes and his entertainment. Thirty-odd years ago the wage-earner used to be called 'the hundred yen husband' as, after turning over his monthly pay envelope, his wife give him an allowance of 100 yen a day for his expenses. The amount has been increased over the years to keep up with inflation but the relationship has not altered.

> The Tokai Bank questioned 545 wives in three large cities and reported in 1977 that six out of ten controlled their husbands' pocket-money after the men handed over their pay packets unopened at the end of each month. The survey showed further that about 16 per cent of the wives charged interest on any extra pocket-money doled out after their husbands had spent their monthly allowances.

> One thing for which I can vouch, some husbands arrange with their firms' accountants to receive part of their salary personally before their wage-packets are sealed and delivered to be taken home to their wives. This practice has been so well established that housewives' groups have successfully petitioned many firms to pay salaries into the employees' bank accounts rather than hand over cash in sealed envelopes to their personnel. Nowadays most companies remit husbands' salaries to bank accounts that wives operate.

> In 1984 the Dai-Hyaku Life Insurance Company surveyed 500 male employees of major business firms, aged 20 to 55. One husband in four had, after that year's 'spring labour offensive', been given an increase in his pocket-money after negotiations with his wife. The average increase was 7.6 per cent, bringing the average monthly allowance to 48 780 yen.

Japanese wives are acknowledged as a power within the home. Does not the person who controls the purse-strings sit in the seat of power? Although they present a low profile, and most confine themselves to their domestic role, their position inside the family is stronger than that of many a foreign wife. The Japanese wife it is who decides what to save, what to spend and how to spend it. The husband will be consulted and encouraged to say, 'We will buy a new refrigerator,' or 'We will take a holiday to Hawaii,' or 'We can't travel because we must give priority to our child's education.' Rarely are his words more than a cloak for his wife's decision. The family depends on her. She controls the children's education which preserves the foundations of Japan's culture.

A majority of Japanese women obtain satisfaction from their management of their homes and their families. They aim to be perfect housekeepers although an increasing number now seek employment to supplement the family income. Especially when their children have grown up and they are no longer bound by the confines of their homes, they may also become involved in outside activities. However, whatever their outside interests, they make sure they do not conflict with their duties in their home and many choose activities that will lead to improvement in their role as housewives. The most that many want from their husbands is a stable source of income.

A nationwide government survey on the status of women, published in 1978, asked 20 000 women and 3 000 men what made their lives most meaningful. The women replied: children 52.6 per cent, family in general 13.2 per cent, occupation 9 per cent and, at the bottom, husbands 2.7 per cent. The mens' choices were: career 43.9 per cent, children 28.8 per cent, hobbies 15.9 per cent, and, again at the bottom, wives 4.8 per cent.

Wives rarely oppose their husbands aggressively. The relationship is one of mutual dependence and is often less 'wifely' than 'motherly'. Husbands are looked after as though they were grown-up children to be pampered like babies.

Most Japanese wives are very conscious that a husband must work to provide for the family and accept that he must spend time after office hours in entertaining or being entertained in order to hold or improve his position in his place-of-work fraternity. Many believe that the later their husbands come home, the more important their positions. I have known husbands stay late at their clubs because if they went home early their wives would worry that the neighbours would think they no longer held important positions.

When a Japanese husband returns late at night, the dinner spoiled, his wife, on her knees in the entrance hall, instead of complaining may say, 'You poor dear. How hard they make you work at the office.' She can see that he is very drunk and the husband knows that she knows. The method is that of judo which uses the opponent's strength for the throw, not the direct aggression of the boxer.

Japanese ladies find they get the best results from their men by flattery. One evening I walked, soaking wet into a bar. To make conversation with a beautiful hostess I commented that it was raining. She said, 'Is that so?' with such apparent admiration that I repeated my statement. She replied, 'Really?' with such praise for my powers of perception that I felt my jacket to make sure that I was drenched and to dispel the feeling that I had made a very clever remark.

The husband's dependence on women is reflected in his need for additional female companionship outside the home. The well-trained geisha and the vivacious bar-girls help wives in the task of mothering the husbands and may also, sometimes, fulfil the wifely role missing in the home.

The mother-in-law remains a power in many households despite the increasing number of nuclear families (those with no grandparent living in the home), now about 60 per cent of Japan's 36 million households. (The figure need not conflict with that of another survey which places 70 per cent of elderly persons living with their children. There could be two or even more grandparents in one home). Another survey says that about three million wives still live with their husband's mothers, mostly in subservience to them, but a growing number of new brides refuse to live with their parents and the relationship between wives and their mothers-in-law has changed substantially in recent years. Mothers-in-law now have occasion to deplore the 'indifference and cold attitude' of their sons' wives and many wives complain against 'the feudalistic, old-fashioned values of living' held by their mothers-in-law. In the old days the wife had to be patient to endure living with her parents-in-law. Today's wives are more aggressive. The mothers-in-law often suffer.

In evaluating the reality of women's lives in Japan the pressure on an unwed mother to abort her baby is an example of unfairness to women. In almost every nation of the civilised world except Japan single mothers can give birth privately. Here, the physician must report the mother's name for every birth and this must be recorded in her civil register which is public and can be consulted by the go-betweens before marriage and employers before engaging staff. The unwed mother has to choose between aborting her child or reducing the possibility of marrying another man in the future.

Undoubtedly Japanese women do not fare well outside the home and the surprisingly large number who work (about one third of the labour force) are heavily discriminated against. The number of part-time workers, mainly women, was recently estimated by the Prime Minister's Office Statistics Bureau to have quadrupled in the previous 20 years. Being paid by the hour, they were said to be less expensive than full-timers and they could more easily be employed or dismissed to match the companies' needs.

Women's average wages are less than half those of men. In 1984 the International Labour Office reported that Japan was the only industrial country in the world where the wage discrepancy between males and females expanded between 1972 (46.5 per cent of men's wages) and 1982 (43.1 per cent). Only about three in a thousand women reach the position of section chief or higher. Although the courts have ruled that discrimination against women violates the Constitution, and some Japanese women have been successful in court actions, a recent Labour Ministry survey showed that about 20 per cent of labour agreements reached between trade unions and companies discriminated against women in setting retirement ages.

Outside the home, consumers, spearheaded by women's groups, do not have political clout when confronted by producers who are more strongly integrated into the political structure. An example of where political power lies is the government's reluctance to free the import of beef and other agricultural products even though retail prices of some foods are about three times the level they could be if strict import quotas were removed.

Although Japanese women play a more dominant role than is apparent on the surface, their position in the labour market is far from satisfactory. More equality of pay and working opportunities and more child-care centres are needed to reduce hardship.

CHILDHOOD TRAINING

Cultures may not be created in the nursery, but established social values are transmitted there. Japanese society has retained its competitive-communist traits from earliest times and adapted them to today's complex society at least partly through the way children are taught. Japanese mothers rear their children to depend on others, not to stand alone in a hostile world.

In Japan the mother aims to appease rather than to discipline the baby's emotions. She enjoys nursing. The breast, available at any time, is a source of mutual pleasure and comfort as well as nourishment. Crying is prevented or stopped by nursing and body contact. The Japanese mother communicates more physically than verbally, fondling, soothing, holding or rocking her baby. Her child comes to fear being alone. It is trained to dependence on its mother. Security centres on the mother's presence.

Many Japanese mothers and fathers share their beds with their babies and their children. It is not unusual for young couples to sleep conjugally only for a year or so until the birth of their first child. When a new baby is born an older child, till then sleeping with the mother, may sleep with the father, or grandmother. Sleeping with parents reinforces dependence as oppsoed to the separateness of individuals. It places strong cultural emphasis on family life and underplays the sexual aspects of intimacy.

Aggressive punishment is exceptional. Within the home the atmosphere is comfortable and non-competitive as each member knows his or her place in the family hierarchy, firmly established by sex and the order of birth. Smaller families and greater affluence nowadays allow mothers more time to devote to their families. This strengthens feelings of dependence at the root of Japanese behaviour.

Japanese parents indulge their young. The child is given a freedom rare in other countries. Etiquette, toilet training and the expression of thanks for favours are patiently taught. By experience, through the mother's quiet perseverance, the child is disciplined to comply with what other people require of him or her. This, not what is 'right' or 'wrong', becomes the yardstick for behaviour. The penalty feared most is the threat of being expelled from the house. Outside the home, as the child grows, he or she must be accepted by peers. Foreign families tend to unite against the outside world. The Japanese family, itself so dependent on others, may reject its own child if it defaults socially. The child becomes self-centred but maturity demands self-discipline.

At the opposite pole was the late Truby King, a New Zealand doctor who believed that from birth babies should be disciplined to the strictest of feeding and toilet routines with no concessions whatever. Truby King played havoc with my generation of New Zealanders.

In Western families the baby is put on to feeding and sleeping schedules. The mother talks to her baby as much as she fondles him. He sleeps alone, his mother frequently out of sight. Often the baby is left in communal nurseries or with strange baby-sitters. He receives material rewards and punishments through the giving or withholding of toys or food. As he grows older, he may be allowed only foods his mother thinks good for him.

Western parents anticipate that their children will have increasing freedom and must, from birth, learn the rules to be able to fit independently into social living. The child is disciplined and may feel neglected, but becomes sturdily individual. Of course, some foreign children are reared with a continuing dependence on their mothers, but our labelling of such offspring as 'still tied to their mothers' apron strings' implies that they are exceptions rather than the rule.

Not till he approaches the harsh educational system is the Japanese child forced to face the competitive world and then every member of the family assists the prospective examinee. The early spoiling is a prelude to the hardest of hard worlds. The child's life-time career hinges on the educational level he or she reaches, not just the university degree aimed for, but the ranking of the university from which he or she aspires to graduate. Graduates from the 'best' universities enter the 'best' places of work. A man's employment and status in later life is determined less by his parents' status than by his educational standard at the age of nineteen when he has taken a job or enters a university.

Progressively from the time he toddles, the Japanese child's studies come to occupy all his days, much of every night, and most of his school holidays. First come examinations to enter kindergarten, then successive entrance examinations for the elementary and higher schools which lead to universities.

Many three-year-olds are sent to coaching schools to help them surmount their first hurdle. To pass entrance examinations more than 25 per cent of kindergarten children and 50 per cent of elementary and high school students attend after-hours private schools or receive extra tuition at home. Many eleven-year-old boys and girls in their last year at elementary school study eleven hours a day, a stint that includes homework and three hours of cramming at high pressure private schools, additional to their regular schools. Their over-protective mothers help by visiting libraries, museums and other institutions to ferret out material to assist their children write the essays they must submit.

In school there is little competition between students. The school or university takes over the mother's role and has an obligation to graduate those it enrols and teaches. Rarely is anyone failed. Education is channelled, not into learning as such, but into preparation for the next school's stiff entrance examination. Japanese learning takes the form of ceaseless memorisation by constant repetition and drills.

Because of the huge number of applicants for the schools which lead to the best employment, entrance examinations are predominantly the one-answer kind for easy marking. Single answer questions penalise originality and measure only a fraction of the examinee's capacity and potential. By some standards the results are excellent. A 1982 study of Japanese and American children's scores on standardised intelligence tests put the Japanese 11 points higher than the Americans and gave 10 per cent of the Japanese an IQ above the average of 130, compared with only 2 per cent of the Americans. Perhaps influenced by these and similar test results many American academics praise Japanese mothers for this scholastic superiority of their children. However, assembly-line education necessitates uniformity and conformity. The teacher does the talking. The students listen. Originality and reasoning are discouraged. Creative minds are not assisted. Schools and teachers cannot experiment with the curriculum, the subject matter, or teaching methods.

> A 1981 survey by the Prime Minister's Office of 1000 parents in each of six countries found only 22.7 per cent of the Japanese parents thought originality and creativity important compared with 74.1 per cent of the Americans, 54.1 per cent of the British, 48.3 per cent of the West Germans and 45.6 per cent of the French.

There are no special classes for gifted or slow learners. Children are not promoted ahead of their age nor are slow learners held back. The stress is on uniformity. It is considered shameful to be even a little different from others. Learning in a broad sense is stunted and consideration of abstract principles stifled, but about a third of all high-school students advance to college about the age of nineteen.

University studies take a minimum of effort and very little thought. Undergraduates are expected to accept what their professors pronounce, not to question and certainly not to criticise. The long series of 'examination hells' through which the young Japanese pass to make the change from dependence on parents to dependence on the place of work have been compared to tribal initiation rites.

The final initiation rite, the examination to enter their chosen place of work, is often less rigorous than the tests to enter the university. The freedom of university life provides undergraduates with an opportunity to run wild but most students' energy and inclinations are soon channelled into membership of clubs which become more important to them than their academic classes. In the clubs they learn to switch their dependency from family to groups of hitherto strangers all groping to belong in their new environment. The seniors in the clubs rapidly teach them the elements of hierarchy and mutual dependence which set the pattern for their conformity when they find their place of work.

At twenty-three years of age university students reach the spring-board from which to dive into their working lives. The transfer of personal allegiance from the family to the place-of-work fraternity is almost accomplished. Throughout their working lives, graduates are able to assist one another by advice and introductions. The utility of their background, however, depends also on their success in climbing the ladder. Those who rise have little time for their less successful classmates who, in turn may be too embarrassed to ask favours of old friends who have out-paced them. The old-school-tie has great advantage if the school has prestige, and alumnae retain their links, but this fraternity is secondary to the one in which they work.

It must not be assumed that the rising generation takes kindly to the post-war rat-race. Children become overly studious or lethargic. The minority accept the system seriously and settle down to succeed, but an Osaka Department of Education survey in 1979 reported that seven out of ten students were dissatisfied with their schooling. They said they could do better but had no interest in trying. The same number had thought about dropping out of school. Indifference to the future was expressed by 80 per cent and six out of ten said they did no homework. This ties in with police reports that juvenile delinquency is at an all-time high. A 1982 White Paper on Youth reported that violence in schools, mostly junior high schools, had increased by a third over the previous year. An Education Ministry survey released in 1983 revealed that 1715 teachers at 657 schools throughout Japan had been targets of acts of violence by students during the previous two years. Such findings could point to change in the future although it must be borne in mind that in all countries at all times only a minority of the population reaches the top, that those at the top control their country, and that despite the rebellious element it is those who accept the school system in Japan who will reach a position to try to perpetuate it.

In later life non-critical submissiveness is required of the pupil. Training is personal, one-to-one, modelled on the earlier parent–child relationship. 'The child is father of the man' and woman. The present educational system perpetuates the traditional system of dependence, cliques, hierarchies and, in short, competitive-communism.

13 Labour

'LIFETIME' EMPLOYMENT

Japanese youths graduate from high school about 19 years of age, or from university about 23. Of the high proportion that continue their schooling through university many graduates choose their places of employment, if they can, after weighing up the benefits they expect to receive through to compulsory retirement around the age of sixty, or older if they become directors. Although the wind of change is blowing, the large companies seldom discharge their permanent employees and permanent employees of such companies rarely change jobs midway. The young graduates expect that for many years their promotion will follow seniority more than productivity, but they hope that, if they show in their work that they have the makings of managerial ability and if they can gain the confidence of their superiors, they will be promoted above their fellows when the time comes. The majority intend to identify themselves with their company and derive satisfaction from belonging to something they feel to be significant. They accept an oppressive system and subordinate their personal interests in return for membership. These employees even hope that the employer will arrange another job for them after their retirement. The first job determines their lives.

'Lifetime' employment gives security, promotes cliquishness, impels conformity and fosters competitive-communism. As it embraces executives as well as lower ranking personnel it influences all company thinking and decision making. However, though widely publicised as a keystone of the Japanese economy, it gives no simple solution to labour problems. Though it plays an important role, it is neither unique to, nor of ancient lineage in Japan. In the bureaucracies, banks, and some large commercial enterprises of all advanced industrial nations 'lifetime' employment has been, and is, standard practice.

The foundations of 'lifetime' employment in industry in Japan were laid as recently as the First World War, when factories were expanding explosively and skilled labour scarce. To hold experienced labour, 'lifetime' security was introduced with company-sponsored welfare services and annual wage increases linked to length of service, but managements restricted these benefits to only a very small, skilled portion of the work force. With life-expectancy short, 'lifetime' employment in Japan's first factories might have effectively lasted a lifetime for the few it covered, but enterprises made little attempt to retain unskilled labour which was readily available and for which employment conditions were not benevolent. 'Lifetime' employment is, in its present widespread coverage, a post-1945 growth.

Small and medium-scale businesses which are the backbone of Japanese industry may promise but cannot guarantee 'lifetime' employment. Large corporations employ 'secondary manpower' – workers who are not acknowledged as permanent. However, a relative shortage of labour in recent years, coupled with the strength of the company unions, has increased substantially the proportion of privileged workers with their employment guaranteed to a pre-decided retirement age. They enjoy a stable job and a stable, annually increased income, unless they are in a structurally unstable industry. Before the yen rose dramatically in value in 1986, they outnumbered temporaries in some large companies and even in some small ones, provided part-time workers, mainly women, were not counted.

Until the introduction of 'lifetime' employment about 70 years ago, Japanese labour was mobile from company to company. Nowadays the 'permanent' industrial worker has been given security, but has little chance to sell his skills elsewhere. He is not a member of a craft union. Wide training within his company gives him competence in many jobs, but makes it difficult for him to fit easily into a specialist position in another. With regular wage increases each year, the longer the 'permanent' worker stays with a firm the greater his advantage to remain. Most accept their situation as giving them more benefits than they would expect by changing jobs. Nevertheless, workers have always moved if they could count on obtaining further and better employment, and times change. Since 1986 many large firms have had to restructure and reduce their work-forces. They make strenuous efforts to re-locate their employees but 'lifetime' employment, which had been so much a part of Japan's economy when labour was in short supply, lost its central role when the growth of manufacturing slowed.

A generation ago, with life expectancy at about 45 years, retirement at 55 justified description as a 'lifetime' for the few workers covered.

The age of compulsory retirement was 55, or 60 in a few companies only a few years ago, but the government set a target that, by 1985, all workers should be entitled to remain in their jobs beyond the age of 60. The target was not reached on time but a large majority of male union members have achieved the goal and most of the remainder have extended their retirement age to 57 or better. However, with a male life-span now of over 73 years, and more than 10 000 000 Japanese over the age of 65, (still under 10 per cent of the population compared with 14 per cent in many Western countries) the words 'lifetime' employment, or even 'permanent' employment could logically be thought a mockery. Employees have 'secure' employment, but I put the word 'lifetime' in quotation marks. Compulsory retirement at a pre-determined age is a part of the so-called 'lifetime' contract. Companies make a large lump-sum severance payment when a 'permanent' employee reaches the pre-determined age limit, but the employee ceases to be part of the fraternity.

Annual wage increases have been as vital to the 'lifetime' system as security until retirement. Although to a growing extent annual wage increases are no longer universally automatic and now ability and responsibility are being taken into account, age and length of service have been explicitly recognised as promotion criteria, a correlation being expected between skill and time with the company. Even this rule is changing and a number of large companies (including Itoh-chu and Japan Victor) now stop automatic annual wage increases at the age of 40, or even 35, beyond which employees must pass tests to be given promotion.

When wages of permanent employees are increased year by year, and especially when recruitment of youngsters is curtailed, costs multiply with an older work force. Besides being costly, the practice produces more mid-level managers than needed. They delay smooth communication between top management and the rank and file and hamper organisational efficiency. Since the 'oil-shocks' from 1973, with world trade slowing down, the 'ageing of employees' and the 'swelling of the supervisory class' have become major problems.

In a contracting economy many mid-level managers become redundant. They are given high-sounding titles and desks close to windows to enjoy the sun while idling, but they cannot easily be dismissed. It has been said (a Japanese projection) that each such under-employed mid-level man costs his company in salary and expenses, such as entertainment allowances and the salary of a secretary, as much as

Y15 million (US $75 000 at an exchange rate of Y200 to the dollar) a year. On this extreme estimate a company could save money if it retired such men with a severance bonus of as much as Y100 million (US $500 000) rather than spend Y150 million keeping them on the payroll for ten years! In fact most retirement payments are dramatically lower. Mitsui & Co. was said, in April 1979, to have inaugurated optional retirement which offered male employees aged between 48 and 52 supplementary grants which totalled around Y3 000 000 per man. (The big trading firm was said to have had about a thousand redundant mid-level employees in the 48–52 age bracket.)

A Ministry of International Trade and Industry survey as early as 1979 reported,

> Many large companies are cutting down on their work forces, centering on employees middle-aged and over. Half of the employers have changed their past 'seniority-based salary raise and promotion systems' in order to reduce wage costs ... Although big companies are stepping up efforts to cut back the work-force, very few dare to resort to outright dismissals which still remain largely a taboo in the Japanese employment climate. Instead, the most common way used is 'loaning out' redundant workers to subsidiaries and affiliates. Under this practice, workers 'on loan' continue to be the employees of the parent company on paper but actually they are destined to finish their working lives at the new place of work .... In extra-large corporations, in particular, the majority of those ordered out to subsidiaries and affiliates were aged 50 or older, and their new jobs in most cases were as salesmen.

In the West governments have been left to look after the unemployed, the old and the sick. In Japan workers look first to the company for security. Low state pensions force about 70 per cent of retirees to take new jobs after leaving their 'lifetime' employment. The gravity of this situation is alleviated to a certain extent by a typically Japanese compromise. If the company needs staff the retiree, having been paid a severance allowance, is retained as a 'temporary' employee at a wage at least one third less than he had been receiving, justified on the grounds that an older man has fewer expenses than a younger one. The company benefits because its wage bill is reduced and 'temporary' employees can always be laid off should the company wish to reduce personnel.

Whatever the terminology, the 'secure' employment system has a profound effect in instilling morale. To any labourer, or manager, there is a world of difference, felt at all times, between a contract of employment for about 30 years and one that the employer can, and in the West often does, break at any moment by giving a day, a week or a month's notice. The Japanese wage and salary earner does not feel that he may at any time be thrown into the street without recompense. 'Lifetime' employment, though neither old-established nor unique to Japan, has in the last 30 years, in spite of its disadvantages, become a show-piece of the place of work fraternity.

'Lifetime' employment presents problems for managements during years of recession but even firms which introduce modifications consider the 'lifetime' employment system, to the extent that it holds trained staff and encourages loyalty, should be retained. The trade unions and their members agree. They are as concerned with the 'permanence' of employment as they are with the amount their members are paid. All aim to preserve the security of the place of work fraternity.

INDOCTRINATION AND INCENTIVES

Whenever possible, Japanese employers choose and train novices rather than engage skilled experts from outside. They employ 'whole persons', not 'hired hands'. They hold training camps for new employees and drill in the company motto which probably embodies a theme such as harmony, faithfulness, effort, sincerity, service or responsibility. (Samples are: 'Ants build a tower', 'Your right to speak lies in your performance', 'Both you and I are managers', or 'Give, give and take'.) Recruits are expected from the outset to work together for the company, not to try to out-perform their fellows.

Imagine yourself, an eager young man or woman on your first day of work in Britain or America. Your department manager would tell you that he expected you to justify your appointment by your personal achievements. How different would it be on your first day in a Japanese company. In Japan you would be exhorted to work wholeheartedly for 'our' company and to do everything required of you for the betterment of the company – to submerge yourself in it, not to hold your post by your personal results.

Employee training and re-training on the job, planned and carried out on a long-term basis, has a special place as a motivation in Japanese companies. For the worker, the security and satisfaction of being intimately close to a body of fellow-workers is coupled with a mutually shared pride in the results achieved. For the management, a high degree of job interchangeability and frequent transfers give flexibility to cope with technological change and to counter craft specialisation. By holding their employees for a 'lifetime' they also guard against leakage of company secrets to competitors.

Indoctrinated workers accept the introduction of new machinery without struggles to renegotiate wage-rates or for other compensations. There may be apathy when change is called for, but rarely aggressive conflict. Although a worker may remain in one department, within it he may be moved around and may enjoy changes which counteract the boredom of routine work. Not only the feeling of security engendered by 'permanent' employment, but also the system of continuous, but not specialised, training conditions workers to new equipment and to other innovations on the factory floor.

Managements give material as well as psychological incentives to persuade their workers to identify with their firm. They may supply food, clothing and goods from their stores at below market prices. They frequently provide dormitories for their single workers and housing for those who are married. They may give cheap or free holidays, often in the company's own leisure facilities. The low cost partly accounts for the spectacle of employees who see one another all day at work spending their free time with the same companions, but another motivation for holidaying together is the 'need to belong'. The Japanese company can be a family, with its frictions as well as its togetherness. A founder of the famous Sony electronics company has said that a Japanese company is, 'a kind of social security organization .... It is like a family with management responsible for all personnel.' There is no clear-cut division between management and workers.

Twice-yearly bonuses are now part of all workers' expected pay. They are rarely less than two months and not infrequently six months basic salary paid both at mid-year and again in December. They give a psychological impetus to productivity. By being paid as lump sums, they encourage saving and are also a way of holding down monthly wages. Bonuses depend only partly on each company's profit for the period. It is customary to pay bonuses of two month's wages even when the company has incurred losses.

'Lifetime' employment, fringe benefits and annual wage increases are only a part of the system. The vitality of worker co-operation comes also from the subordination of investors to the management which is made up of senior workers. A worker is inhibited if he feels that by working harder or by showing his foreman a better way to perform a task he is merely adding to the income of some 'capitalist' who takes the additional profit for himself. A worker has no such inhibitions if he feels that, by making his company more successful, he will gain by greater security of employment, as well as additional personal income and fringe benefits and greater prestige in the eyes of his fellow-workers. These incentives give the Japanese worker pride in his work.

Discipline is strict, but managers tell the workers what changes are proposed and explain why they are needed. Workers participate in shop-floor decisions, and joint responsibility is of paramount importance. Routine circularising of information around the company, far more thorough than in other countries, gives employees a knowledge of what is going on and a consequent sense of belongingness. Management and employees come to know each other well. Communication becomes so smooth that management can use fully each employee's experience and skills. There is communal dependence, shared by all who participate as 'permanent' employees, their business and personal lives woven together. Managers know they also are workers and that the company benefits by giving incentives to the whole team.

The West takes almost single-minded account of the individual's ability. Japanese communal customs subordinate individualism to team work and minimise the division between managers and workers.

An American multinational with a large and important subsidiary in Japan, International Business Machines (IBM), gives its workers lifetime job security, generous pensions, group insurance, medical coverage, and payments for children's education. However, IBM has emphasised the individual, not the group, with job security for the competent and dismissal for those who fail to achieve the standards demanded. At one time some superiors in IBM's Japanese corporation supervised subordinates' activities while seated behind them. This horrified the Japanese who arrange desks alongside and facing one another so that everyone sees everyone to reduce feelings of dominance and submission. The Japanese feel that to fraternise only when off duty is hypocritical. When interviewing new candidates IBM Japan chose them for defined vacancies, profession by profession (public relations, accounting, finance, salesmanship, etc.). The individual was rarely moved from one kind of work to another. IBM Japan now follows the Japanese practices more closely than it did. For instance it has adopted 'blanket' recruitment, dividing staff into only two categories, engineering and all other work, rather than hiring for more specialised positions.

SECURITY

A most visible and enduring characteristic of Japan's social structure, as a motivation at the place of work and in the home, is security. Some say this security is the system's greatest strength, but it has seeds which, if they sprouted, could jeopardise the whole fabric of today's society. Perhaps most of the people, most of the time want security, but does everyone, all the time? Safety from violence, freedom from poverty, and the comfort of not being alone must not be underrated, but they have their prices.

Safety from violence enables citizens to walk the streets and to sleep at home without fear of being molested or robbed. Communal living has proved a most potent weapon against crime. It is backed by small police stations dotted close to hand through all cities, towns and villages and implemented by the compulsory registration of everyone's 'permanent' and 'current' places of residence and of all births, deaths and marriages. With much criminal activity fraternalised, individual crime plays a minor role. Communal interdependence suppresses individual outbursts against the system and prompts an interest in neighbours' activities. Mutual dependence bolsters social restraints which add to the security of life, limb and property. There is something in the twin Japanese views that everyone is responsible when society's rules are broken and that a person who apologises is likely to accept the law and observe good human relations in the future.

The security of employment that removes fear of starvation embodies general acceptance of the broad understanding that we must produce in order to consume. Security of livelihood carries a heavy price. 'Lifetime' employment can be lifetime bondage. Immobility of labour frustrates the finding of alternative employment. By co-operation and compromise and by refraining from asking why, conflict is diminished, but everyone knows his position and lives within the salary level and working conditions of his grade at his spot in the hierarchy.

Then there is the security of not being alone, of belonging, of being accepted on intimate terms by one's mates at work as well as one's family at home. Human relations at work are respected, but all individuals must conform to the opinions of others and carry the ever-present fear that anyone who does not follow the communal dictates may lose security and become an outsider for whom the system has little room.

These securities given by the Japanese clan and fraternal system have advantages that must not be underestimated but, to quote any Japanese, nothing is all good or all bad. Is one secure if one is dependent on insiders and uncomfortable, insecure and cautious with all outsiders? Institutionalised security undermines self-confidence. We must bear in mind the positive and negative aspects of security when looking for the motivation of the Japanese people and the endurance of competitive-communism.

'WORKAHOLICS' AND 'ECONOMIC ANIMALS'

If we visualise an alcoholic as an addict obsessed with a craving which takes total priority in all his, or her, thoughts and actions, then a 'workaholic' conjures up a similar image. The totality of the concept is misleading, particularly as a picture of the younger generation in Japan. One can enjoy alcohol without being an alcoholic. If we have to labour, it is less irksome if we can find satisfaction in our tasks. Japanese workers have been instilled with an interest in their jobs and an understanding of the necessity to work.

About a third of Japan's industrial workers, or their fathers, have been born on farms. Those who raise food know the necessity of working in order to live. In earlier centuries the Japanese subsisted on the verge of starvation. In time of famine population growth was restricted by 'weeding' (infanticide) among the poor. With the development of industry a hundred years ago an oversupply of labour held wages at a subsistence level. Staring starvation in the face, and indoctrinated by government and employers with the virtues of frugal living, the workers bowed to the inevitable and made the best of necessity. The older generation still accepts work as an inherent part of life. Though this attitude is not the exclusive prerogative of the Japanese it differs from that of most Western industrial workers who have a 'work is punishment' ethic ingrained by the long, bitter struggle that witnessed the development of capitalism.

Japanese employers have shown skill in providing satisfactory working conditions, encouraging team spirit, and discouraging individualism. Workers trained over the years to identification with fraternal objectives become anxious for their fraternity's success which they couple with their own. They become less concerned to know why a particular task should be carried out than to be assured that the job should be done in the interest of the fraternity.

Are the Japanese more loyal or more hard-working than other people? Most show a greater interest in the product of their work and in the success of 'their' firm than is usual in the West. Most, when asked their jobs, will respond by saying they work for the XYZ company rather than that they are a truck driver, or a typist. While such answers indicate the strength of the communal system, the Japanese worker is extremely practical and extremely conscious of his personal financial requirements. I have been employing Japanese staff for more than thirty years and some have stayed with my firm from the time they left university more than a quarter of a century ago. Others have left when it suited them. In my experience, Japanese loyalty can switch from one company to another if there is financial advantage. Though they may work longer hours, they do not work harder than Westerners. The communal place-of-work remains the core of Japan's economy, but it should not be thought that workers are unanimous in accepting their places in fraternities by enthusiastic choice. They bind themselves for self-interest when they see little alternative of earning a better income by moving. They are stern materialists, not addicted 'workaholics'.

This is not to say that Japanese do not work hard or that they are not loyal to their companies. Deeply-rooted habits of dependence, on-the-job training, and participation in decision making, preserve the work-ethic particularly amongst older workers. A majority do not feel themselvs to be small, insignificant and replaceable parts in impersonal machine-like organisations. They identify with their jobs, pride themselves on their industriousness, and are even able to work 'with a feeling of happiness'. Necessity and indoctrination have produced diligent workers a majority of whom still find fulfilment in their roles and derive security and social support from fraternal employment.

Although they are this-worldly and materialistic, the epithet 'economic animals' distorts Japanese traits. Apart from their great artistic and intuitive skills the Japanese are more dependent on human relations than most peoples. To hold their jobs they are 'economic' in putting their place of work above family, friends and outsiders, but only people who indulge in the belief that they can gratify themselves without any obligation to add to the world's goods or services should isolate the Japanese as 'economic animals'. Aren't we all? The sting and the warping of the epithet is the irresponsible word 'animals'.

A new generation of Japanese employees has in recent years shown itself capable of following Western precedents. It exemplifies the experience of other countries that better paid workers are more militant than badly paid ones in fighting for higher wages and better conditions. Unless there is the desperate shortage of jobs of the past, the attitude of the present generation could with surprising speed move from the present communal role towards that of their individualistic American and European counterparts.

A 1980 government poll of 3000 youths between the ages of 15 and 19 gave no indication that the rising generation will be addicted workaholics. Over 70 per cent put personal interests and hobbies above work or study. The same proportion viewed study purely as a means of developing personal ability. Over 60 per cent thought Japanese society offered nothing worth striving for.

However, despite the indications that young urban workers are beginning to lose the traditional habits of hard work and thrift, the place of work is still the core of Japanese life and 'lifetime' employment a foundation stone of Japan's economy. But, in looking to the future, it is a cautionary thought that the strong edifice of clan, fraternity and cell is built on a sandy foundation – the suppression of individualism, an absence of choice.

TOTAL QUALITY CONTROL

Japanese Quality Control Circles, much talked of around the world, are part of a whole system, not slapdash or imposed dictatorially. Throughout Japan there are said to be some 300 000 circles embracing two million workers. They meet regularly to discuss their quality control and production problems. The 'quality control' name came to Japan from America during the Occupation with a method for inspection for defective goods being supplied to American troops fighting the Korean War. Since then the concept has changed completely. It is now Total Quality Control (TQC).

The philosophy behind TQC was summarised by the Japan Productivity Centre at its foundation in 1955:

1. We believe that improvement in productivity eventually leads to expanded employment opportunities. Temporary redundancy

should be dealt with to the extent possible by re-allocation, thus minimizing the risk of unemployment.

2. We believe that specific steps for improving productivity should be studied by joint consultation between labour and management.

3. We believe that the fruits of improved productivity should be fairly distributed among management, labour, and consumers. (It is worth noting that shareholders were not mentioned.)

Kohei Gohshi who was instrumental in founding the Japan Productivity Centre and who headed it for its first 25 years said:

Twenty-five years ago, we started the productivity movement with a conviction that its ultimate goal should be to improve the welfare of employees. No matter what management may do, the physical productivity will not improve unless people working in the company are willing to work and gain a feeling of doing an important share of work. In those days, Japan was eager to introduce scientific management from the West. But we felt that management involves not only technology but also human heart.

While the efforts for raising productivity have been mostly directed to the technical side in the West, our efforts have been directed to raise the level of satisfaction of workers at the place of work. In other words, it is not enough to simply try to manipulate productivity. We have to deal with the heart of people. Thus I believe that the issue of productivity should be introduced with a cultural approach.

Inspection of finished goods should not be necessary if they are properly made. TQC mobilises all resources within the company and passes policy decisions from top management through middle management and first-line supervisors to the workers on the shop-floor. It activates the entire organisation in such a way that everyone understands and participates. Inspection takes a very low priority. The target is to ensure better products by analysing manufacturing problems through detailed, statistical study and isolation of what has caused a defect. Good products come only from good processes at every stage. TQC aims to eliminate trouble at its source whether it be in the original design or specification of the end product, or the material or the equipment and labour used all the way through to sales and service. Workers are encouraged to take a personal interest in their work and to use their brains as well as their hands.

TQC incorporates the entire functioning of the company. It leads to high quality goods and lower costs. Workers can take pride in producing goods which bring praise to their place of work and to themselves personally. TQC embodies consumer benefit and helps the whole company as satisfied customers are its best salesmen. Workers' morale improves when high quality goods are produced and customers are satisfied. The personal pride of the craftsman in his product has been created in huge, very modern factories despite conveyor belts and repetitive work.

Westerners who flock to Japan to learn the magic of quality control circles should reflect that almost all quality circles that were started without top management commitment to introduce TQC are said to have failed. Quality control is not effective if confined to the creation of circles of workers on the factory floor. These circles are only a part of the concept. Quality control at all levels of management and administration must be put into practice. Managers must think of themselves as part of a team, not as opponents of the workers below them.

In addition to quality control circles, industry benefits enormously from workers' suggestions. The Japan Productivity Centre reported in 1987 that the workers' participation rate in Japan (1983 figures) was 58.3 per cent and in the United States (1978 figures) 14 per cent and the number of suggestions per worker in Japan 14.7 compared with 0.15 in the United States. The ratio of suggestions adopted by the management in Japan was 75.9 per cent and in the United States 24 per cent. The economy achieved by 305 Japanese companies was 261 100 million yen and the rewards to workers in 467 Japanese companies 11 800 million yen. The huge number of suggestions came from very active management encouragement (some say positive direction) in generating suggestions and in giving them serious consideration.

It is also worth noting that, in Japan, there is currently another major topic of discussion and activity considered to be as important as quality control and to be a part of it. The new cliché, Small Group Activities, has yet to be popularised in the West but it is said that, in Japan, any book with this title can sell 5 000 copies at its first printing so great may its merits be. It is public acknowledgement within Japan of the cell as a vital segment of the Japanese fraternity. Small Group Activities are now given a legitimate place in Japanese management theory and practice.

TRADE UNIONS

Many English words adopted by the Japanese have come to mean something essentially different in their new home. 'Trade union' is a clear-cut example. Professor Robert Ballon of Sophia University, Tokyo, has gone as far as to say, 'Trade unions in the Western sense do not exist in Japan.' Labour–management confrontation does not follow the Western pattern.

Trade unions in the West, based on crafts or industries, not the place of work, their members scattered in many companies, are structured and function very like typical Japanese fraternities. In contrast, most trade unions in Japan are not independent fraternities. The 'National' unions are dominated by their member unions, all-embracing place of work organisations which are, at the same time, factions within their bigger corporate fraternities.

'Company union', also, does not have its full Western meaning. The term 'enterprise union' instead of 'company union' may help reduce misunderstanding. Just as Japanese people remain egoists while subordinating themselves to their fraternities, so also the autonomous enterprise unions in Japan retain their identity while part of their company community. Members of Japanese enterprise unions enjoy a sense of security without accepting subservience that may be felt in management dominated 'company unions' in the West. They are determined that their enterprise must protect its workers' interests.

After the end of the Pacific War, when trade unions were first legalised, workers swarmed into them. They were radical, but the Occupation quickly crushed a general strike. Few craft unions emerged. Almost all unions, while affiliated to national organisations, settled into company frames, each centred and mainly concerned with its single industrial enterprise. Although the Japan Seamen's Union and the Japan Teachers' Union are in effect craft unions based on individual membership, the majority of National Trade Unions are federations of company unions.

Only about one third of Japan's labour force is organised. 'Temporary' workers are excluded from Japanese company unions and are either unorganised or members of separate unions.

For all 'permanent' workers, white-collar (below managerial grade) as well as blue-collar, membership in their company unions is automatic, not optional. Permanent employees become, or expect to become, section managers after about 15 years' work. When promoted they cease to be members of the union. If they have been leaders in the union and have acted to the management's satisfaction, they have improved their chances of becoming top executives in their company in due course. There are few professional union leaders but many (about one to each 300 to 400 members) full-time paid officials.

To prevent factional control and to obtain a consensus most Japanese unions require a very large quorum, up to two-thirds of the membership, for their general meetings. The meeting chairman is not the president or an executive of the union, but is appointed for the one meeting. The union executives at the general meeting are, in principle, defendants of their policies and their actions. In practice the union chairman, 'from behind the screen', is likely to dominate the chairman of the meeting.

Japanese management claims that it is years ahead of the West in accepting labour participation. In a 1981 survey, 74.1 per cent of the companies surveyed replied that they had one or more board members who were at one time union officers and 16.2 per cent of all the board members under this survey were identified as having had union leadership experience when they were young. Labour participation in management is advanced in Japan, and the high proportion of ex-trade union company directors reflects this, though the company orientation of the trade unions should be taken into consideration when making comparisons with other countries.

The 'lifetime' employment system arose because of the employer's need to hold his skilled labourers who were demonstrating with their feet that they would change their jobs if they were offered higher wages. The post-war trade union movement has had to fit itself to a 'lifetime' employment system and, for the decade after 1945, a huge surplus of low-paid workers. It has adjusted to meet its obstacles. Within the enterprise unions it has not been practical, in negotiating for wage increases, to distinguish between the tasks and skills of its non-specialist members. Instead of fighting for sectional interests, each enterprise union has generalised its claims towards equal pay increases within its company, taking into account its workers' jobs, ages, and numbers of dependants and also to relate its members' wages with the level paid by other companies.

The National Federations of Unions have less authority over their member unions than in the West. They have also been weakened by continuing confrontations on ideological lines between competing National Federations. Frequent attempts in post-war years to organise a united labour front have failed. Nevertheless the National Federations have devised an effective way to improve wages by joint struggles for minimum standard wage increases. Starting in 1955 they initiated an annual 'Spring Labour Offensive' as the core activity of the labour movement. It reflects the national mood in its timing, its cliquish organisation, its rituals, and in the results obtained.

Each year the 'Spring Offensive' opens with a series of demands, economic and political. The National Federations, in the words of Tadashi Hanami, 'feel responsible for the welfare of the working class, the fate of the Japanese nation and peace in the world'. However, the 'Offensives' are customarily settled with agreement only on wage increases.

Although the joint struggle is co-ordinated at the national level and embraces all workers, the wage goal and the timing is not uniform for every affiliated union. The underlying strategy is that several of the large enterprise unions within each industry should co-ordinate their bargaining by harmonising their wage demands and negotiation schedules under the guidance of their National Federations. When strikes are called their date durations are synchronised, but even though the struggle is combined, the actual negotiations are within each enterprise, not nationally centralised. The unions of the medium-sized and smaller companies participate in the 'Offensives' as junior partners. The first battle is against the major industries. After agreement at this level the unions of second-ranking companies fight with the aim of obtaining the same settlements as those made with the big companies.

It is not always easy to recognise the subtle, completely un-Western ways in which some Japanese struggles manifest themselves. Japanese unions, to gain their objectives, aim to embarrass their managements, not to damage their companies financially. Strikes are but one tactic and are neither their most representative nor their most common weapon. Other forms of action include work slowdowns, working to rule, partial strikes, sit-downs, leave-taking *en masse*, pasting posters over windows and premises, and wearing arm-bands. Under Article 1, Section 2 of the Trade Union Law it is legal for trade unionists, provided they are not too violent or excessively threatening (a provision which is interpreted very liberally by the courts), to enter a manager's office, to shout, to threaten, to demand and to bargain. They may refuse to leave the office even though this is repeatedly requested by the manager.

Trade unionists show greater dependence on their own enterprise union than on their union's nation-wide federation. They are aware of their importance as workers and that their security of employment may be in jeopardy if their company does not survive and grow. Enterprise unions effectively reduce the conflicting interests of management and labour, but it is an illusion of some Western observers who study large companies to think that Japanese industrial relations are free from conflict. Bitter confrontations are rare in large firms but common today in small ones.

A dual wage structure before 1950 disappeared but is emerging again. Between the 1960s and 1970s, in an expanding economy, there was little differential in incomes. However, since the mid-1970s differentials in incomes have grown markedly between employees of government and large businesses and those who work in small enterprises; in declining and expanding industries; men and women; white and blue collar workers; and between industrial workers and farmers. In addition a huge differential in wealth has arisen between those who owned land before 1950 and those who did not. (The cost of buying land and building a house has risen to at least eight year's salary.)

With harmony a social virtue and confrontation a social evil, Japanese society expects individuals to suffer in silence so, if compromise fails, it shows deep-seated grievances. Managements exert great efforts to avoid confrontations, but they may not recognise dissatisfaction building up below the surface until it erupts violently.

Serious conflicts are not settled by logic or objective arguments or reference to statistics or to universal standards and precedents in the Western way. An appeal to the emotions of the parties is effected through an impartial and respected mediator and conciliation mechanisms which rely on mutual trust and understanding. The adjudicator must command the respect of both sides and is more a mediator than a decision maker. His aim is harmony through compromise and great faith is put in him by both sides. He must save everyone's face and the parties must save his. Though settlements may not follow the precepts of Western logic, the Japanese method could bring a new dimension to 'impersonal' Western industrial relations.

Unions and their members aim to expand their firms' incomes. By increasing the size of the pie they expect to receive more pie themselves. The trade union movement is active in Japan even though totally different from its Western counterparts. It perpetuates the 'lifetime' employment system by making it very difficult for management to dismiss labour. It has not opposed the Quality Circle development. It has done well by its members but it uses its power carefully, always aware of the importance of not crippling industry.

Part IV
Japan in Recent Years

14 Japan's 'Economic Miracle'

Japan's industry and commerce have grown at a spectacular rate in the last 35 years. Her cars, cameras and electronic equipment have penetrated people's lives from America to Zambia. The high quality of her products and their competitive prices have raised Japan to an imposing position, centre-stage, in world economic affairs. At the time of writing her economy is the envy of the world. She influences international market movements and is, of course, influenced by them. Japan's development has been described as an 'economic miracle'. Bewildering, fabulous and stupendous it may have been, but not miraculous. The foundations of post-war expansion were laid a hundred years ago.

In 1868 the Emperor Meiji was restored to the throne of an undeveloped agricultural country divided into many semi-autonomous domains. Japan had just met the West face to face. She was poor with surplus labour and few employment opportunities except on her overmanned farms. Dependence and co-operation within small agricultural communities was everyone's life in a social system which had remained undisturbed by foreign intervention through all its history. To defend its country, the new government financed the building of factories and set out to absorb the technology and industrial experience of the imperialist powers that threatened her. The seeds of Western industrialism fell on fertile soil. Factories took root and flourished, though not without the growing problems that all new things encounter.

The Japanese are proud people, but stern realists. To resist foreign colonialism they humbled themselves at the feet of foreign teachers and studied hard. To be accepted by aliens they wore Western clothes some of the time and the wealthy installed a visitor's room with chairs and foreign flooring and furniture in their native houses. They introduced a European parliament and European legislation, but only the surface of Japanese lives changed. Within the broad framework of 'foreign' laws which they had put on the statute books, judges made their decisions in accordance with traditional concepts of justice. Periodically, when pride surfaced, foreign teachers were sent home and Japan flexed its growing muscles by challenging and defeating her neighbours on the battlefield.

The eager workers who flocked from over-populated farms to the cities took whatever jobs were available, but vacancies in the new factories could not absorb them all. Those who found no work in the cities returned for sustenance to communal dependence on their poor families on the land. The majority of the population remained part of and dependent on small 'extended-household' agricultural units.

Came the First World War. While the European powers battled they could not supply the markets they had built world-wide. Japan (and America) stepped in and prospered. In Japan the huge expansion of her industries created a shortage of skilled labour. To hold their trained men factory managements adopted the role of the agricultural household and offered lifetime employment, but only to a small proportion of their trained work-force. Unskilled labour was still plentiful and low-paid. Japan's economy grew tremendously but her heavy industry, built to preserve the state, not for profit, was the tool of the military. Her commerce was in labour-intensive products. During the depression years of the 1930s Japan filled a world-wide market for cheap priced goods.

Japan supplied what the market would buy at prices it would pay. Her tea cups retailed around the globe for a few pence each. The cups were shoddy, their handles broke off at the slightest provocation. When I came to Japan shortly after the termination of the Pacific War, I was amazed to find that she had for centuries been producing very high quality ceramics. I asked the president of a famous pottery how Japan had achieved global stigma as a manufacturer of trash.

'It's quite simple,' he explained. 'The Woolworth's and other large buyers would come with huge orders, but the prices they offered were unbelievably low. We told them that they would have to pay much more for decent quality. They insisted on their prices. We wanted the orders and supplied them. They knew and we knew that the goods were trash but they seemed satisfied and kept coming back for more. We believed that foreigners were uncultured and could not afford respectable quality goods.'

By 1940 Japan had become a powerful, well-equipped industrial nation with a large, experienced work-force.

THE POST-WAR 'MIRACLE'

At the end of the Pacific War in 1945 Japan lacked food and the raw materials of industry – iron ore, coking coal, oil, cotton, wool. Almost all her factories had been destroyed. Her rice crop could not feed her population. Relief supplies from the Allies barely held starvation at bay. Repatriates from her prewar colonies and demobilised soldiers and sailors made a huge, ragged army of unemployed. Even those with regular work found their wages submerged in a tidal wave of inflation. (In the three years from the end of 1945 to 1948, taking 1945 as 100, the wholesale price index for 1948 reached 3750.) Life was grim but, looked at with hindsight, the ready availability of cheap, able labour and the chance to rebuild factories with the newest and latest technology and equipment, were great advantages. The world shortage of goods of all sorts provided an insatiable market for anything Japan could export.

Between 1945 and 1952 the Japanese people were subservient to an Army of Occupation which practised democracy when it was not enforcing military discipline, confusingly and unexpectedly. For survival the Japanese accepted the whims of foreign businessmen – 'buyers' they called all alien traders. Very slowly industry, depending at first on cheap labour, took root but there were few signs of solid recovery.

Came the Korean War. The United States needed vast supplies for her troops and made strenuous efforts to harness Japanese manpower. Any manufacturer must gain if he has cheap, industrious labour readily available, is helped to obtain raw materials, is given financial backing, and has a huge profitable market. During the Korean War, the price of steel doubled and every ton that could be produced was eagerly bought. Financed by the buyers and encouraged by the high prices their output commanded, industry sprang to life at incredible speed.

At the end of the Second World War the Occupation authorities had taken strenuous measures to dismantle the pre-war giant trading and industrial enterprises – the *Zaibatsu*. These efforts to break up the excessive concentrations of economic power proved only partly effective. A regrouping and merging of the divided companies began when the United States turned to Japan for supplies during the Korean War. The tight family ownership and control of pre-war days was destroyed but with, perhaps, a little less co-ordination at the top, the monsters have been restored to ever greater size.

Holding companies are not legal in Japan, but mutual interlocking of shares by major corporations is widely practised and directors are swapped between affiliated companies.

An overwhelming volume of Japan's commerce is now in the hands of huge, aggressive trading companies, each still fighting to expand its exclusive preserve, its tentacles holding large slices of Japan's economy and spreading world-wide. Each supplies raw materials to the factories it dominates and sells much of their output through its wholesale, retail and export outlets. Nine of today's largest trading companies handle the bulk of Japan's current imports and exports. Each is centred around its own main bank on which it relies, although it is encouraged to use other banks also.

The heart of the rehabilitation was the banks which were left largely unscathed by the Occupation. Each major bank has been, and is, the nucleus of its group of huge industrial and commercial enterprises – one reason behind the high proportion of corporation borrowing from banks in relation to shareholders' capital.

In contrast to European and American practice, Japanese companies depend more on short-term loans from banks than on raising capital from other sources. Short-term borrowing by Japanese corporations in relation to their capital has been about six times as high as that of American businesses. Corporations have recently tended to decrease the proportion of their borrowing from banks and to increase their capital by issuing more shares, but the proportion of their capital to their borrowing remains much lower than in the West. In consequence the banks take a close interest in all their customers' financial transactions and in their profitability to satisfy themselves that they are not at risk. As a Western businessman I am made very aware of the meticulous concern my Japanese banks have in the profitability of my company. They are just as interested in my transactions as in the very adequate collateral security they require when making a loan. However, the banks, unlike Western shareholders, are not concerned to receive high dividends. Their requirements are that their loans are secure and their interest paid.

In the early post-war days the banks treated as prime security Letters of Credit received from abroad to cover export orders and they lent clients they considered reliable up to 80 per cent of the Letters of Credit amounts. This cash advance was used to buy the raw materials and pay the labour needed to make and export the goods. I built my business from this ready source of capital.

The high rate of corporate and personal savings of the Japanese has been a major factor in their country's rapid economic growth. From the outset of industrialisation the Meiji government actively encouraged savings by propaganda which declared 'Luxury unpatriotic' and 'Extravagance our enemy' and created a nationwide network of Post Office Savings Banks which made depositing easy. Personal thrift was promoted by the deeply ingrained Confucian precept of frugality and by a lack of social services that forced saving as a necessity. The people, though desperately poor, had to save for emergencies, the inevitable costs associated with birth, sickness, marriage and death. Today in Japan's more secure society, personal saving is encouraged by the bonus system which the employer has to budget as a part of salaries, but the staff receives twice yearly in large lump-sums. Emergencies have still to be guarded against. The costs of marriage and of education to open the way for improved job opportunities for their children have increased. The Japanese maintain the habit of saving. In 1986 their net annual savings were about 17 per cent of the gross national product compared with the United States' about 5 per cent, but personal savings of salaried workers are increasing slowly and will diminish as the population ages. As a general rule in all countries older people save less. It is the young who have the need for saving.

Savings by commerce and industry have contributed to the national well-being as effectively as personal savings. Guided by the banks, profits have been retained for each company's use and dividend payments minimised. Company directors' salaries are not geared to profits and they do not receive incentive bonuses or shares, so they are not stimulated towards quick profits provided their companies stay in good financial health with their shares high-priced on the stock exchange. Relieved of incentive or pressure for large dividends, company directors are able to place a large part of their profits into reserve funds and to take a long view when planning and budgeting.

Manufacturers in other countries try to eliminate middlemen between their factory and the final consumer. Most Japanese industrialists have concentrated on manufacturing and have left the selling to specialists.

Shortly after the war's end, I represented the Hong Kong Government in Tokyo. One morning a Japanese manufacturer put a cloth sample on my desk and asked if Hong Kong used the material. When I enquired why he asked, he said that his factory had escaped Allied bombing and was able to start production if he could find a market for its special product, the red flannel that he was showing me. He

said that over many years his factory had made millions of yards, all
for export, but he had no idea of what country or countries the cloth
had been going to. 'We delivered to the trading company's warehouse
at Yokohama,' he explained. 'They sold it and put on the shipping
marks and now the trading company has been broken up. I don't
know what country to offer to.' The post-war situation is not dissimilar.

Situational responses play an overwhelming part in Japanese
business. Supply and demand determine pricing more markedly than
in other countries. The Japanese sell at the best price the market
will take, not at a price based on the cost of production.

When I visit a manufacturer in Japan as a buyer and ask for a price
on an item in his sample room, he does not immediately make a
quotation even though he has been selling the product for years. He
picks up the little wooden frame with beads on which experts add
and subtract as quickly as on an electric calculator, and he fiddles
with the beads before coming up with a price. This gives him time to
take account of the competitiveness of the market in the country I
am buying for, but of greater importance to his calculation are the
state of his order book and the size of my potential order. If he is
short of work to keep his factory going he will quote a cheap price.
As his order book fills, his price will be higher.

During the Korean War the world was short of steel. My company
was selling to New Zealand and other markets. Each morning we
received cables asking for prices on specific quantities of mild steel
bars, angles, sheets. We rang each of the five giant steel mills and
received offers, good for forty-eight hours, on each of our enquiries.
On one morning we would find Yawata cheaper on bars, Nippon
Kokan cheaper on angles and Fuji cheaper on sheet and we would
cable the cheapest offer accordingly. The next morning, or even the
same afternoon, we would receive cables with further enquiries and
we would again obtain offers from each mill. Rarely would the same
mills be cheaper on the same items. As they reduced their unsold
capacity so they revised their prices day by day, sometimes hour by
hour. At the same time British and Australian steel mills maintained
their prices unchanged but could only supply a fraction of the orders
they received. After about a year, the building and bridge contractors
in New Zealand were still receiving about half the steel they needed
from Britain or Australia at an unchanged price of about £40 a ton.
The balance of their needs they bought from Japan at prices which
had escalated by small, constant increases, to about £90 a ton. When
the Korean War ended and steel prices fell the Japanese mills, still
equating their prices with the quantities they were making and the
potential orders as they came in, had made such profits that they
could sell cheaper than the British and Australian mills.

As they are selling to 'outsiders' (at home as well as abroad) each
fraternity's first loyalty is to itself. All are extremely conscious of

the value of established relationships, and they exhibit remarkable reluctance to do business with a 'new face', but they expect their clients to understand that alterations in the market justify increases in prices. Even though long-term contracts have been signed, to Japanese businessmen a new market situation justifies an amendment in the terms of the contract.

That Japanese decision makers are concerned with the 'market share of their products to the exclusion of profits' does not stand close inspection. Japanese companies must make profits, but they can take a long view. They are not pressed by shareholders to make huge, constant profits. In using the term 'market share', misconception may be reduced by substituting the word 'sales', the test of all business success or failure. Maintaining turnover is particularly important to Japanese manufacturers because of difficulties in reducing their work-force, and expansion has great cost advantages since, with payment by age, youth is more productive per unit of wages. (In the West, being by the job, costs are not reduced by an influx of lower-paid young workers.) Of course, all manufacturers everywhere should aim to increase their sales (market share) to obtain the benefits of increased turnover which can lead to cost reductions by giving longer machine runs, cheaper raw materials, lower interest rates on borrowings, lower overheads and more scope in selecting labour. Japanese industry is geared to expansion, to sales growth, but not to the exclusion of profit.

Every businessman would like a market share large enough to put him in a monopoly position with its opportunity to dictate his selling prices, but in Japan the Fair Trade Commission frowns on cartels, or companies, with more than 60 per cent of a market.

The Japanese manufacturer aims for the benefits of large-scale operations and for a larger market share but, at the same time, he does not neglect the basic need to make a profit. To achieve low production costs, the optimum benefit of large-scale production, or just to establish any new product, the Japanese are more prepared than most foreign managers to work on low margins, particularly in the short term while they fight to sell, that is to obtain a share of the market. They seek a high 'market share' and take a fairly long-term view of the profitability of a product line, but they do not neglect the necessity of making profit. The shareholders may not be vocal, but the banks are hard task-masters.

In addition to supplying what markets want at the highest prices they will pay, the secrets of Japan's successful industrialisation from immediately after the war were a huge supply of low-paid educated labour available for her growing industries, the youth of the population, government assistance, the availability and rapid adaptation of imported technology and the propensity, coupled with the necessity, to save. Profits from high prices have been ploughed back into capital investment. With the most modern plant, equipment and technology, costs of production have become lower than in countries struggling along with outdated machinery. Wages have risen but, because of the surplus of labour for two decades after the war, lagged below those in Europe and America. The government was not saddled by heavy military expenditure. A drain on the public funds, subsidies to farmers on whom politicians depended for election, contrasted with negligible provision for welfare and defence. Speculation drove up land prices and rents. For years it was considered irrelevant that the enormous industrial growth was at the expense of overcrowding in the cities – housing shortages, crammed transport and pollution of air and water. Manufacturers were given priority over consumers.

Continuing recruitment of young workers from schools and universities kept the proportion of low-paid workers high and the companies' total wage-bills low. It was not in a company's interests to dismiss trained staff during short depressions while a resumption of high growth was expected. Keeping workers employed during slumps led to greater loyalty, improved discipline in the factories, high quality products and quick deliveries. It also resulted in overproduction, heavy competition, sales at a loss, and complaints of dumping in foreign markets.

Some of Japan's successes are the result of a series of historical events that she has used to the full and benefited from enormously. It must be reiterated that she took full advantage of her opportunities. From 1945 the other advanced industrial nations had the same market to absorb their output. They did not seize so wholeheartedly the chance to modernise their machinery and to improve their productivity to compensate for their handicap of more expensive labour. They did not exploit the consumer by raising their prices to give themselves extra capital with which to jettison old machines and replace them with more efficient ones.

Past circumstances cannot be counted on for the future, but Japan has built a very strong industrial and commercial base from which to handle the needs of the changing world markets. Her ability to seize an opportunity and her tremendous skill in manufacturing and selling are well established.

15 Stone, Paper and Scissors

'Japan Incorporated' as a label conveys correctly the united front the Japanese clan achieves in dealing with foreigners, but gives a facile impression of a binding organisation with absolute control centralised in the hands of a single chairman and board of directors, each with his responsibilities clearly defined. There is no such rigid, formalised 'Japan Incorporated', with centralised, autocratic authority. In practice there are three competing centres of power: bureaucrats, politicians and businessmen. The absence of unified dictatorship has prompted use of 'competitive-communism' as an alternative label while 'clan' depicts the binding frame of Japan's self-centred racial exclusivity more aptly than 'Japan Incorporated'.

If any sector of a nation calls for single, overall, unified control it must be the armed forces. Let those who cling to the idea that there is a Japan Incorporated with coherent and centrally controlled economic policies pause to glimpse at Japan's Self Defence Forces. In April 1979 the Asahi Shimbun reported,

> No one at the Defense Agency seems to know what division of it makes defense strategy. As a matter of fact, the Defense Agency makes none. Strategy is mapped out by the three branches of the Self-Defense Forces – Ground, Maritime and Air – in the form of their annual Defense Plans. The annual Plans, while keeping in view the Joint Staff Council's varied scenarios of an attack on Japan, are based entirely on the respective defense capacities of the trio and on their respective reasoning. Taken together, they are like a three-piece crazy quilt, each piece the work of a different person.

Similar comments on un-coordination were repeated in 1984 in a report, prepared by the Peace Problem Study Council serving Prime Minister Nakasone. It stated that there was no co-ordination between the expansion and improvement plans of the three Self Defence Forces. If Japan's defence strategy is not centrally controlled can we expect overall, centralised management of the whole economy?

Japan is un-incorporated, not just because the nation has no autocratic board of directors and functions without legally structured organisation, but also because the Japanese prefer informal relationships which do not set out rights and duties in inflexible detail. The communal structure within the clan, though at all times an uneasy coalition of cliques with competing interests, binds equally as strongly as a written constitution. An incorporated entity is not the only frame in which individuals join for their common interest. Partnerships and cartels in all countries can be as binding as corporate structures and just as effective in making a common front against outsiders. The Japanese go one step further than Westerners. They make the preservation of harmony and human relations as binding as legal partnerships even though they are 'unincorporated'.

The complex and often contradictory reality at all levels is a marriage of competition with co-operation between bureaucrats, politicians and businessmen. The marriage is sometimes calm, at other times tempestuous. While preserving a united front to outsiders, only the partners know what is really happening between them at any time.

BUREAUCRATS

The Japanese civil service compares closely with its counterparts elsewhere. The official establishments of modern countries resemble a Japanese fraternity to such an extent that one could visualise, quite wrongly, their being from the same stable. All enjoy in common the close, protective association of 'established' insiders who treat outsiders, if not with disdain, at least as being no part of their exclusive fraternities. Each establishment has its own small competing cells as loyal to and dependent on intimates as on their large fraternity. Let us confine our attention to the Japanese version of the government establishment.

The ingrained belief that government bureaucrats are superior beings with favours to bestow dies hard in Japan. Until the end of the Pacific War the acts of the government and of its officials transcended the law. Despite political change Japanese civil servants still retain more than the memory of their traditional power.

Elite bureaucrats come from the cream of the educational system, gain most of their experience in a single ministry, and become highly experienced in the law related to its functions. They have prestige and most are honest, efficient and, because of early retirement at 55 years of age, vigorous. They often have great advantages over their Cabinet Ministers who rarely hold their positions for more than one or at most two years which gives them little time to establish more than general control over bureaucrats with 'lifetime' specialisation.

The number of high-ranking civil servants who 'descend from heaven' to influential positions in commerce and industry reinforces close links between business and bureaucratic circles. (The National Public Service Law puts a two-year ban on employment of officials by private firms related to the government ministries with which they had been connected in the five years prior to retirement, but 267 ranking ex-government officials found employment with private firms in 1983, a fairly typical year.) Both sides know a great deal about the other and maintain close contacts. The employment of retired officials can facilitate managerial co-operation between bureaucrats and businessmen. However, just as the daughter has her name removed from her family register and inscribed on her husband's at the time of marriage, the retired civil servant ceases to be part of the bureaucratic fraternity and joins a company fraternity at the time he is re-employed. Very close human relation links remain, but the insider/outsider alliances change.

By some alien standards Japanese civil servants would be given a clean bill of health, but bureaucrats in semi-government agencies and occasionally those in important ministries are sometimes abused by the press for accepting 'gifts' from businessmen and for misappropriating the taxpayers' money. For the year ending March 1984 the Board of Audit uncovered 182 cases of doubtful accounting by government ministries and public corporations involving 17.1 billion yen.

In May 1980 an audit of the semi-government Nippon Telegraph and Telephone Public Corporation (NTT) discovered massive misappropriations estimated at 145 million yen in fiscal 1978 and 123 million yen in fiscal 1979. President Tokuji Akikusa and other NTT officials were disciplined for falsifying business trip accounts and spending the funds for the officials' own entertainment. Akikusa resigned a few months later 'to take responsibility' and, in August 1983, the 17 000 managers of NTT accepted group responsibility and decided to repay 480 million yen that it was decided they had used personally.

While earlier aircraft industry scandals had disclosed bribes paid by foreigners to politicians, it was not until the Kokusai Denshin Denwa (KDD) case in late 1979 that the public learned of domestic pay-offs to high level officials. KDD (not to be confused with NTT which holds the domestic telephone monopoly), at that time a public utility firm under the supervision of the Posts & Telecommunications Ministry (P & T), held a monopoly of international telegram and telephone services and reaped huge profits each year. The P & T approved increases or decreases in KDD charges and appointed KDD executives. In March 1980, following the earlier arrests of his juniors and of two senior P & T civil servants, Manabu Itano, president of KDD from 1975 till the scandal broke in 1979 was arrested on suspicion of embezzlement. In 1979 two assistants in his office had returned from Europe with nearly $50 000 worth of goods which they grossly undervalued for duty purposes. When challenged by Customs officers, they confessed that the goods were for their KDD superiors, not for their personal use. It transpired that KDD entertainment expenses in the previous three years had exceeded 5000 million yen and, of this, abut 2000 million yen had been used to purchase paintings, antiques, furniture, jewellery, accessories and department store gift certificates. The balance had been spent on entertainment, 'going-away presents' and tickets for parties to 'encourage' politicians. It was implied that Itano bribed the bureaucrats and politicians to hold his position and to influence them not to order a reduction in international telegram and telephone charges when the value of the yen had fallen to about 200 to the dollar while KDD continued to bill at an exchange rate of 360. It was also alleged that Itano had syphoned off some 'gifts' and entertainment expenses, at least to the value of ten million yen, for his personal use. In 1984 the court found Itano guilty on a number of charges.

Such cases may have dulled some armour but have not reduced the authority of the bureaucratic establishment. Westerners think of civil servants as wielders of red-tape which clogs private enterprise. The Japanese think of them as functionaries who make and implement the rules which make for communal harmony.

POLITICIANS

In post-war Japan democracy, as a political theory, reflects a foreign concept which proved its military superiority in the Pacific War. Into a society which does not accept individualism, the forms of Western democracy have been adopted and adapted by necessity and as a voluntary reaction against the monopoly of power by an unacceptable and unsuccessful wartime dictatorship. During the Allied Occupation the Japanese installed a method of government similar in form to Western democracy. The parliamentary system has become accepted as a suitable form of government.

The Japanese use the word democracy constantly, but their interpretation of the term is not ours. In the West we overlook the inherent contradiction between the inviolability of the individual's rights and the absolute power of the majority. Whereas our democracies claim to protect the rights of the individual, the Japanese aim to preserve a benevolent social order, their traditional communal system. To them democracy should take account of the peoples' needs and rule by unanimous consent. Political decisions should be reached by compromise to achieve the greatest good for the clan as a whole. This is difficult to achieve for the whole national clan as it involves wide consultation to ascertain the consensus. Hierarchy plays its part. The larger the population the greater the dominance of top members and the less 'democratic' the decisions. Nevertheless the Japanese expect a strong spirit of compromise.

While the opposition parties in post-war years have not shown the ability to unite, or had the leadership and policies, or the financial backing to take over the government, they have prevented or delayed the legalisation of many conservative policies desired by the governing party. In the early post-war Diet, members 'fought for democracy' with their fists. Nowadays, when the governing party rejects their demands, the Opposition members leave the Diet. The government then negotiates until a compromise is reached and parliament can return to normal functioning.

Just as the clan, though it unites against aliens, is too large to be consistently a single-purpose fraternity, so also Japanese political parties present a unified front only towards their opposition. The political parties, each an uneasy coalition of conflicting 'fraternities' (in the political arena correctly called 'factions') have not fused into single fraternities. The governing Liberal Democratic Party (LDP) is broken into warring factions which compete vigorously against one another. So also is its largest opposition, the Socialist Party. Factions have emerged to their present strength as effective, flexible political organs. Each clusters around a man who has leadership ability, political skill, the ambition to become Prime Minister and, above all, the ability to raise funds. Faction leaders fight to become their Party's president and thence, if their Party has a majority of seats in the Diet, Prime Minister.

Cabinet Ministers are not chosen by the Prime Minister because of loyalty to him or his policies. He invites into his Cabinet a selection from his party's factions who oppose him and his faction. His rival faction leaders accept this as a matter of course. The Prime Minister needs their co-operation to hold the Party together and they need to hold high office while they await their opportunity to overpower him and step into his shoes.

Wide public criticism of factions has forced successive Prime Ministers to declare their intention to abolish them. They even, from time to time, go through the motions of liquidating their own faction (Fukuda in 1976 and Miki in 1980). Factions change in leadership and size, but so far no major ones have been disbanded. They remain the core of the parliamentary party system. Competition among them has prevented a monopolisation of power.

Unfortunately, to be elected a Member of the Diet, the aspirant or his intimates must spend a vast sum. A few public-spirited citizens like Yukio Ozaki two generations ago and Aiichiro Fujiyama more recently, have frittered away their personal fortunes, but they were exceptional. Most aspirants for political office expect to be reimbursed and rewarded. The system encourages opportunists with special interests, not idealists. Politicians compare money with fire. 'It has great usefulness as long as it is controlled.' Payments to political parties and to individual politicians are astronomical. Official figures (yen 69 300 million in 1976 to yen 167 600 million in 1986 and still increasing) are misleading as they do not include all contributions.

Members of the Diet receive about 17 million yen plus transportation and communication costs and allowances for two secretaries, but the money needed is said to be about ten times the stipend in non-election years and several times more than this in election years. To cover this huge expenditure funds were said to come from four sources: the Japan Federation of Economic Organizations (Keidanren) from whom the LDP was said to have received about 12 000 million yen in 1986; the LDP faction leaders (at that time, Takeshita, Abe and Miyazawa, each aiming to succeed Prime Minister Nakasone) were said to have built up, in 1986 in reserve for the 1987 power struggle, about 9 000 million yen; then there is the collection of funds which are not publicly accounted for (the so-called *Uragane*-money, below the surface). In addition to these three sources of funds the Diet Members have also, individually, to raise publicly-accounted funds.

The number of voters who cast their ballots at elections is an impressive 70–80 per cent of those eligible, but there is little grass-roots participation by the general public in selecting, financing and active campaigning for candidates. Support organisations, created and financed by the would-be Diet Member, not by his constituents, combine the disbursement of funds with personal allegiances, backstage intrigues and manoeuvres which extend down from the politician to the individual electors. The politician attends, in person or by proxy, weddings and funerals and shows his congratulations or his sympathy by monetary donations. Voters are more concerned with personalities than policies which appeal most when they offer some concrete advantage to the electorate. Some voters expect to be financially compensated, 'to show appreciation', for their ballot rather than to contribute to supporting their candidate.

In 1979 one candidate in Chiba prefecture was reported to have spent 400 million yen. In 1984 the National Police Agency announced a much lower figure (125 million yen) that it had uncovered for vote buying in the December 1983 election for the House of Representatives. It had found 4235 cases of election law violations (90 per cent for vote buying) involving 7732 people, 686 of whom had been arrested. In many cases, one vote was priced at 3500 yen. One unsuccessful LDP candidate in Osaka had spent 20.14 million yen to buy votes. These figures are, of course, only those related to cases prosecuted by the police and they do not imply that all candidates violated the election laws or that all voters received payments.

The largest political scandal of recent years has been the charge that Kakuei Tanaka when prime minister had received 500 million yen (about US $1 400 000 at the exchange rate at the time) from the Lockheed Aircraft Corporation. The Lockheed pay-off became public knowledge in February 1976 when Carl A. Kochian, former vice-president of the Lockheed Corporation, deposed at a Senate hearing in the United States that in 1972 he had been forced by his company's Japanese agents, the Marubeni Corporation, to pay the 500 million yen to be passed to the then prime minister, Tanaka. Tanaka resigned as prime minister in 1974 when unsavoury land deals were exposed. In July 1976 he was arrested, with his secretary Toshio Enomoto, on charges of violating the foreign exchange control law in relation to the Lockheed payment and he was formally charged the following month with taking the 500 million yen bribe in return for his help in the sale of Tri-star jets to All Nippon Airways.

Local papers wrote that Tanaka could almost certainly have evaded conviction by pleading that he had received the money as a political donation, a ploy that had succeeded on a number of occasions. (The number of such cases are said to exceed the number of seats in the House of Representatives – 511 – but only 30 of those questioned ever faced indictment and most of those were acquitted by sticking to the 'political contribution' line of defence.) Tanaka chose to insist that he had not received the money even though the evidence showed that he had received it.

The court proceedings against Tanaka dragged on for over a decade during which time other defendants in the case were found guilty and sentenced. Despite these long-drawn-out court proceedings Tanaka was for many years re-elected to the Diet and his faction grew remarkably in size. During this period he was acknowledged to be 'king-maker' within the ruling Liberal Democratic Party. When Prime Minister Zenko Suzuki resigned in 1982 it was said that the new prime minister Yasuhiro Nakasone was elected because of the support of the Tanaka faction. As proof of Tanaka's 'king-making' power, Nakasone appointed to his cabinet and to equally important posts in the Liberal Democratic Party six men of the Tanaka faction or friends of Tanaka including the Minister of Justice, Akira Hatano, the Minister of Home Affairs, Sachio Yamamoto, the Minister of Finance, Noboru Takeshita, the Minister of Health and Welfare, Yoshiro Hayashi, the Minister of Construction, Hideo Utsumi, and two key executives, the Chief Cabinet Secretary, Masaharu Gotoda, and the Chief Secretary of the Environment Agency, Matazo Kajiki.

It was thought by many that Hatano might have used his position to close the case following a precedent set almost 30 years earlier. In 1954 the police had arrested the secretary-general of the governing party, Eisaku Sato, later to be prime minister, for implication in a so-called 'ship-building' scandal. The Public Procurator's office had indicted Sato for receiving the money and informed the Justice Minister, Ken Inukai, who informed the Prime Minister, Shigeru Yoshida. Yoshida instructed Inukai to order the indictment cancelled. Inukai did so and resigned the following day. To return to Tanaka, in 1985 he suffered a stroke. His power behind the political scenes lessened while he lay semi-paralysed in hospital. The case against him dragged on, but he did not lose his power behind the scenes until 1987.

Political platforms have for years given prominence to 'administrative reform' and the 'elimination of corruption from politics' but such planks are neither controversial nor ideological. That they should be important is a sorry reflection on Japanese politics. Ideologies play only a small part in political decisions.

To see the Japanese economic system as a whole, the roles of bureaucrats and politicians must be linked with the part played by businessmen.

BUSINESSMEN

Though few industries are nationalised, neither bureaucrats nor politicians have been adversaries of business. The need for government assistance was obvious when, in 1945, the shattered economy had to be rebuilt, but the fundamental policy had been inaugurated seventy and more years before when Japan was under the threat of colonisation by Western nations. Industries were then created by the government to defend the country, not for profit. It was not until they were established and profitable that the government handed them over to private entrepreneurs.

The bureaucracy, with the encouragement of some politicians, has uncritically associated business efficiency with large-size units and, over the last century, has favoured the big businesses which it has been instrumental in creating. Since the units are so large, officials can negotiate with them more readily than if there were more, smaller businesses. On the other hand, the business fraternities, when it suits them, are large enough to oppose the bureaucracy. At all levels businessmen treat bureaucrats and politicians as necessary evils with considerable power which it is their function as businessmen to resist if co-operation would jeopardise their profits.

Japanese businesses enjoy the efficiencies of large-scale production and the teamwork of entire organisations which do not have to syphon off the bulk of their profits to their shareholders. Of equal or even greater importance, managers are not hobbled by market uncertainties to the degree suffered by their Western competitors. All markets are unpredictable. Every business venture is always at risk from changes which may be beyond its control, but the Japanese manager reduces his risks in advance by gaining the commitment of his entire organisation, his bank and his government before he starts a new enterprise. If the market turns sour he has their combined support to reduce his insecurity. He can plan long-term counter-measures without having to spend all his efforts to overcome his more immediate difficulties.

STONE, PAPER AND SCISSORS

In Japan children and adults play a game also popular in other countries called 'stone, paper and scissors'. Contenders expose their hands simultaneously and with the fist clenched (stone), or the hand flat (paper), or two fingers extended (scissors). Each gesture overcomes one of its opponents and loses to the other. In describing the management of their country, some Japanese liken the power structure to the game. Businessmen they call stone, officials paper, and politicians scissors. Significantly, they do not include labour as an active participant. Labour's interests would appear to be thought of as part of the businessmen's stone, not a separate power.

In post-war Japan bureaucrats are not at arm's length from the leaders of commerce and industry. Government policy has been exercised through an 'administration of consent', sometimes called 'sponsored capitalism', somewhere between direct government control and complete freedom for commerce and industry. The policy and intentions of the government bureaucracy are shown by formal and informal consultation. 'Administrative guidance', a popular but not a legal term, may be thought of as 'regulation through inducement'. It includes giving information and concessions, combined with warnings, to influence business towards voluntary co-operation with a minimum of friction and coercion.

Officials do not control and are not controlled by big business. Some bureaucrats may treat businessmen arrogantly, but they rely on them for information and for co-operation and, perhaps, for lucrative employment on retirement. Decisions hinge on human relations and the power balance, case-by-case, between officials, politicians and individual industries who argue and co-operate at a person-to-person level. Japanese laws generally are broadly-worded statements of principle not spelled out precisely. Interpretation, which may be as important as the law itself, is in the hands of officials who, at discussions in their offices, may give only formal information. In more relaxed surroundings, to a person he feels trustworthy, an official may explain, or hint at, specific ways to follow the law.

Until the late 1960s the government provided strong import restrictions and export incentives to key sectors and to promising infant industries. Favoured industries, at first steel, shipbuilding, electric power, coal and fertilisers and then petrochemicals, automobiles and computers, were given preferential tax and depreciation treatment, loans on favourable non-commercial terms, duty-free equipment imports and protection from import competition.

It is widely thought that the bureaucracy has been and is the dominant power in policy making. Officials, if they are able to achieve unanimity within their own ranks, have the advantages of secure jobs, long experience, knowledge of the law and a traditional aura of omnipotence. One critic has said that if we compare the management of the economy with a dramatic production, the bureaucrat is the playwright, stage manager, producer, director and public relations officer for the play and politicians nothing more than the leading actors. Such a generalisation neglects the fact that most dramatic productions reach the stage only when financed by producers whom the critic seems to have underestimated. The parallel also breaks down to the extent that many politicians are graduates of the civil service and have mastered as much background detail as the bureaucrats they work with in policy-making committees, and that business employs many ex-bureaucrats qualified to act on its behalf in writing the scenario and the staging and action of the play.

Equally important, the bureaucracy does not always have a united front. The Foreign Ministry cannot always persuade other ministries to implement promises it has made to alien governments. While the Finance Ministry may aim to control inflation, other ministries may permit price increases in industries under their control. The Ministry of International Trade and Industry (MITI) may wish to relax import controls on dairy products, meat or citrus fruit but is opposed by the Ministry of Agriculture and Fisheries. Without a single national goal and agreement on priorities, ministries with different targets have difficulty in reconciling conflicting aims and have even greater problems in holding the co-operation of businessmen and politicians.

Whether or not MITI has been 'the headquarters of Japan Incorporated', its influence and power is great. It recommends equipment installation, production and prices. Working with business federations and their many consultative committees, it agrees on guidelines to mobilise and deploy resources, but the management of the economy has to take account of competition in its many forms. Not everyone would accept it as gospel, but a recent policy declaration by one of its senior officials stated,

> MITI takes the stand that the government should never do any more than to guide the private sector .... Many people tend to attribute the strong competitive edge of the Japanese industry solely to Government-initiated measures to support the industry. They are, very simply, over-estimating the Government policy measures. The key factor has been the intense competition among private enterprises in the domestic market.

Politicians have power, but they are swayed by day-to-day public reaction to their pronouncements and political factions fight each other bitterly. The voters, who do not feel called upon to pay their candidates' electioneering expenses, expect favours from their Diet members and judge them by the benefits they bring to their electorate. Without the voters' financial support the candidates turn to those who feel that, by contributing money, they will be rewarded if their candidate is successful. This leads to some unholy alliances between politicians and their main source of financial support, the business community. Huge contributions must influence the politicians' relations with big business and blunt their political scissors. At the same time, Diet members have a loud voice in promoting and appointing bureaucrats who, in turn, are in a position to give assistance and guidance to the business community.

The business executives, the bureaucrats, the politicians have no power to make unilateral decisions and have them carried through. If an industry agrees on what it wants, bureaucrats and politicians will consider proposals seriously, but this is equally true of all countries with the difference that Western governments, while sometimes helping ailing industries, rarely think it their duty to support strong ones. These they tend to leave to their own resources. For a hundred years Japanese bureaucrats and politicians have taken an active interest in supporting businesses with potential to grow and have been much less enthusiastic in aiding failing industries unless convinced of their powers of resuscitation.

When the public mood and the interests of labour combined and the whole country had the single-minded goal of economic growth – the expansion of exports and control of imports – bureaucrats, politicians and businessmen worked together with a minimum of friction. The result was in effect, an 'Incorporated Japan', achieved in spite of the factionalist, competitive spirit on which the economy thrived. Consensus, never easy, has become more difficult now that the country's needs have diversified. Co-operation to meet foreign competition can always be counted on, alien business must benefit Japan, but internally demands have grown for an improvement in the quality of life, control of pollution, better housing and transport. In a period of slow growth and contracting markets traditional administrative guidance is less effective in curbing industries than it was when helping them along the swiftest paths to expansion.

The management of the economy may well be likened to the stone, paper and scissors game when the clan is without an overriding goal.

16 Is Japan a Closed Market?

THE JAPANESE MARKET

Business in all countries tends to follow established lines between companies who know one another well. Japan carries these routines far beyond their limits in the West. Clan and fraternal interrelationships may create almost insuperable barriers against 'outsiders'. Business and personal relations closely intertwine. Creating and maintaining intimate association with buyers is difficult and time-consuming. Masaaki Imai has written,

> Of course, maintaining friendly relations with customers is an important prerequisite in conducting business anywhere in the world, but it is all the more important in Japan. While a Western manager considers his relations with customers in terms of a contract, a Japanese manager considers his contract with customers in terms of his relations. In other words, the contents of a contract may be interpreted flexibly in view of the importance of maintaining good will. A Western manager may think that the customer should deal with those who come up with better products and offer better terms and conditions than their competitors. That is to tell only half of the story, however. A little more effort in maintaining pleasing relations with a customer can produce a surprisingly favourable outcome in a business deal.

Imai has also written,

> Hiroshi Torigoye, president of Bausch & Lomb–Japan, recalls the difficulties they encountered in developing new accounts when they started selling soft contact lenses for the first time in Japan. One of his salesmen was finally successful in opening up an account. On his first visit the eye doctor had gently brushed him off, saying, 'We have been using your optical instruments for years, so we know that they are good. But as far as soft contact lenses are concerned, we have been using conventional contact lenses, and there's no need for us to use your lenses.' The salesman talked to several nurses (paramedical assistants) when they were not too busy and tried to make friends with them. He also talked to the doctor's wife. (In Japan, the management of a clinic is usually left to the doctor's wife.) Next day, he went back to the clinic and came to know better the work procedure. He went into the kitchen where the doctor's wife was preparing a meal, kept her company and listened to her fond subject

– cooking. He also kept company with her little son who just came back from the kindergarten. When the son wanted a toy, he took him out to the nearby store and bought him one. The wife, of course, was very pleased with the baby-sitter, and later suggested, 'My husband has no time to listen to you and learn about your products in the daytime. Why don't you come back again after dinner?' So, he went after dinner, and this time the doctor listened to his detailing. When his presentation was over, the doctor said, 'I can't use the new products right away. But why don't you try them on our paramedical assistants and see what happens?' On the third day, the salesman fitted several assistants. Their reactions were all favourable. He made a deal with the doctor . . . . Says Torigoye 'Our customers look at the frequency of the calls made by our salesman and judge whether we really mean business. If our salesman makes a call more often than our competitors, he is regarded to be more "sincere". For the same reason, I am expected to call on our more important customers a few times a year.' Therefore a salesman often calls on his customers just to show up – even if there is no need to discuss business. Only after many such calls, and only after he has been thoroughly familiar with everybody in the clinic, can he be accepted as a member of the 'family' clinic, and can establish a long-lasting support. Torigoye recalls how his competitor lost their account when one of their customers moved to a new and larger quarters: for an eye doctor to open a new clinic is an experience of a lifetime, and for someone who's been invited to attend to the house open ceremony to be absent is unforgivable. It so happened that the day before the opening ceremony, there were railway strikes, and their competitor couldn't come, while Torigoye drove all the way from Toky to the far-off city to keep his promise. It was a mark of his sincerity, and very soon his competitor lost his account with this eye doctor.

It is probably no exaggeration to say that Japan is the most difficult and competitive market in the world and if a company is successful in selling in Japan, it should be successful anywhere. It may even be said that part of the success of the Japanese in selling to other countries comes from their training in their own complex market with its meticulous standards and attention to the whims of fickle and fastidious consumers.

The Japanese open offices in every country they trade with. Local businessmen are flattered. The Japanese learn the market and prosper. Similarly, an overseas firm with the capacity to do worthwhile business should have its own staff permanently based in Japan. The alien representative on the spot shows the Japanese that his firm is serious about entering the market. He encounters and may learn the handicaps not to be expected in other countries. For example, when a Japanese organisation replaces a representative in

London, or New York, or Paris, clients accept the new man in his predecessor's place as a matter of course. Company relations are not disturbed. In Tokyo the alien who is leaving will introduce his successor, but the new arrival may be regarded with reserve by his Japanese opposite numbers until they have got to know him as a person. This may take one, two or even more years. The shorter the time alien head offices keep their men in Tokyo the less productive their work. As their own men cannot be expected to understand Japanese ways in the short time usually allocated for their stay, there is also advantage in the appointment of a non-Japanese firm, apart from an accountant and a lawyer, with long business experience in the country as a permanent consultant. Foreign manufacturers could also adopt the Japanese practice and concentrate on manufacturing, handing the importing and exporting function to mammoth trading companies in their own countries.

The overseas manufacturer who treats Japan as just one more market and who is not prepared to make very special efforts is unlikely to expand his sales.

The management of business in most parts of the capitalist world is geared to making the largest possible profit in each accounting term in order to pay shareholders as high a dividend as possible. A key to Japanese competitiveness in all markets, including their domestic one, is that they have no such compulsion. The non-Japanese company should subordinate short-term windfalls and be prepared for losses when embarking if it can expect solid gains after the early years. Operating costs are high. The company will find that many sales are, in effect, made on consignment as unsold goods may have to be accepted back without charge. It may be opposed by Trade Associations which link its potential customers with competing manufacturers and wholesalers through long-established 'human relations' based on years of working together. It may have to cope with rebates to retailers which have become customary in some trades.

A company wishing to do long-term business in Japan must pay great attention to after-sales service and to maintaining an adequate supply of spare parts. Selling some goods requires as many service engineers as sales engineers. Japanese employees must have pride in the product and not lose their morale by having constantly to apologise to customers for delays in deliveries, for the absence of urgently needed spare parts, or for faulty goods.

Demanding consumers complain about things which have nothing to do with the function of the goods. Quality and service follow rigid lines. Goods have to meet Japanese taste in all respects. Packaging to meet the consumer's tastes is most important and explicit instruction manuals are often needed.

Japanese customers request so many detailed specifications of products and data on test results that it could seem they intend to manufacture an item, not buy it. While this may sometimes be the case, it is more usually an insatiable Japanese need to feel confident that a mistake is not being made in purchasing. It does not follow that the figures and charts and diagrams supplied by the manufacturer will be understood. They may only be the equivalent of elaborate packaging, but they must be given. Packaging is very important in Japan. The American Chamber of Commerce in Japan in a White Paper published in February 1980 reported:

> Buyers of manufactured goods in Japan, who typically do not or cannot maintain large inventories, insist on absolute reliability of supply. Blanket customer service is routinely expected, and may include design modifications to suit each customer. Foreign consumer goods, too, generally require alterations to suit factors peculiar to Japanese demand .... Safety and quality are stressed in Japanese government standards and regulations that cover industrial product specifications in detail. But in many cases these criteria are not closely aligned with internationally accepted standards.

Against these obstacles, many overseas companies have been, and are, successful in Japan. They have studied the market carefully before entering it. They have learned its customs, found the most appropriate sales channels (direct selling to retail is not simple, as many have found to their cost), and have discovered and motivated good staff. The distribution routes are long and complicated, the result of traditional practices, and the many firms and people involved. Selecting the right selling channel and personnel is vital. They have studied Japanese cultural values and tested local response to their products. Very often they have got lucrative results from items that were not necessarily very popular elsewhere. If their company's name is world famous they may find this an asset they had not realised and often of greater value than the trade names of some of their goods. The Japanese are eager for new things that meet their taste and of a quality they can count on.

GOVERNMENT CONTROLS

As if the commercial hurdles to be jumped by the overseas businessman were not enough, the Japanese government had, until quite recently, a single, simple economic policy of expanding Japanese industries. Growth was the national aim. To achieve it, the government virtually closed the home market with official import prohibitions and less obvious but very effective non-tariff barriers. With full bureaucratic support, and without fear of competition from overseas manufacturers, factories established new production lines and employed more workers.

For three post-war decades the Ministry of International Trade and Industry strengthened the economy by helping in negotiations for securing basic materials. By stringent import controls and preferential treatment in taxation and financing, it strengthened corporate competitiveness and promoted exports before opening Japan to foreign competition.

If, for instance, import had not been prohibited, foreign cars would have engulfed the market. Japanese car makers would not have been able to build their production to the high volume that enables them now to sell at cheap prices.

While government obstruction played a very large part in keeping the Japanese market effectively closed, it should not be forgotten that import restrictions are by no means unique to Japan. Even while paying lip service to free world trade, all nations have taken, and still take, steps to protect their home industries. During the last decades alien governments have persuaded the Japanese to enforce official export quotas or to arrange 'voluntary' quotas on very many goods including, for example, steel, textiles, bearings, cutlery, colour TV sets, cars. However, though not peculiar to Japan, controls of imports, by their extreme severity, have evidenced a difference of substance between the ways of Japan and of Westerners.

The position has changed dramatically. Much of the market is now effectively closed on solid economic grounds as Japan produces better or cheaper than overseas manufacturers. Import licensing and non-tariff specification controls have been slowly liberalised. Foreign cars have become relatively freely importable, but can no longer expect massive sales.

Non-tariff barriers have been a constant cause for complaint by overseas businessmen. They make take the form of restrictions on procurement by semi-government corporations; or loans to an industry at preferential interest; or quotas; or customs valuation procedures and approvals; or labelling requirements; or exacting product testing to health, safety and other specifications.

In the last few years, Japan has taken impressive liberalisation measures particularly in fields where her goods are now highly competitive and no longer need protection. Import controls have been reduced to a limited number of items, mainly agricultural products.

> Japan still shows a united front in curtailing the import of fruit, meat and dairy products from America, Australia and other countries. On the surface the issue is simple. To protect her farmers almost total prohibition has been enforced. Domestic prices are at levels as much as three times higher than they would be if there were no restriction on imports. The consumer has been ignored. Over the years, negotiations, even threats (New Zealand, for instance, said that Japanese fishermen may be excluded from her waters), have not yet changed the position. Greater liberalisation is, however, coming. Even rice imports are being seriously considered.

Foreign exporters, though with less justification than formerly, still complain that for each inch a tariff barrier is lowered a non-tariff barrier is raised by two inches. Let us put more recent changes into perspective. Back in June 1979, to discuss non-tariff barriers with alien businessmen, the *Shukan Asahi* held a meeting in Tokyo with American, British, Canadian, French, German and Italian Chambers of Commerce representatives. The following examples of non-tariff barriers at that time were cited:

> The European Community representatives said that data tests conducted on chemical products, medicines, agricultural chemicals and cosmetics by internationally known testing laboratories in Europe were not accepted in Japan and the products had again to undergo complicated tests in Japan. In addition to the costs, in some cases as long as four years passed before the results of the Japanese tests were known, a period during which it had been alleged similar products had been put on the market by Japanese manufacturers.
>
> Instead of naming colouring and other additives that were prohibited, the Japanese regulations listed those whose import was permitted thereby automatically excluding products which were in common use in other countries but not in Japan.
>
> To meet government regulations to import soap into Japan, a firm was required to have a laboratory and to employ a laboratory technician.
>
> The Japanese authorities wanted French mineral water to be boiled and another regulation required sausages to be boiled to 120° which would effectively kill all taste.

Alien chartered accountants had difficulty in being admitted to practice in Japan whereas Japanese chartered accountants, if recommended, had no similar hurdles against their practising in the United Kingdom.

Import of some European cars had been prevented because of stringent and inflexible regulations about the colour and size of tail lights.

The January 1979 report of the Jones Task Force of the Subcommittee on Trade of the United States House of Representatives' Ways and Means Committee on United States–Japan Trade had stated, 'Because of the relatively small number of auto imports, Japanese Government requirements that result in extra engineering, manufacturing changes, and paper work, have especially heavy impact on the pricing and sale of foreign autos .... To meet a number of Japanese requirements, US autos landing in Japan must undergo extensive reconstruction which increase costs by $1000 or more.' The report added that, 'Many of the Japanese Government's regulations seem of highly dubious value or subject to arbitrary inspection decisions.'

Since then the Japanese Government has been taking further steps to improve and simplify Japan's import standards and inspection procedures. The import inspection of electric appliances has been simplified and the testing time reduced from about a year to about two months. The Health and Welfare Ministry has been studying plans to simplify the import procedures for medical drugs and cosmetics, and the Ministry of Transport for cars.

In January 1980 the Japan–United States Economic Relations Group, popularly known as the 'Wisemen's Group', reported to Japanese Prime Minister Zenko Suzuki and to United States President Carter that:

In terms of tariffs and quotas, the Japanese market is as open as the American market for comparable manufactured goods. In terms of government procurement practices, foreign investment rules, entry of services, and procedures of standards, inspections, and testing, Japan's market is not as open as the American market and more needs to be done to liberalize market access in Japan's own national interest. There are special difficulties for foreign business in Japan from more intangible factors such as administrative procedures, traditional business customs and mores, and cultural and social barriers to foreign influence.

Progress has since been made in reducing non-tariff barriers, but the practice has not been completely abandoned. On 11 March 1982 the American Chamber of Commerce in Japan made public a report based on a survey of 495 of its member firms to which 147 responded. The survey was made to bridge the credibility gap between foreigners who insisted that trade barriers still existed and Japanese spokesmen who asserted that the Japanese market was open. The report may be summarised as follows:

Banking. Almost all of the twelve banks responding to the survey said they were adversely affected by foreign exchange controls, and more restricted as to the services they could offer in Japan than in the US. Most of the banks also felt that the restrictions were either 'not equally applicable to Japanese counterparts,' or 'were equally applicable but were more limiting as to US banks.' A majority also said that the volume of their business was limited, and that Japanese banks were either not similarly limited or less severely limited. The banks also complained of an inability to acquire Japanese banks, restricted access to Bank of Japan rediscount funds, Bank of Japan limits on their foreign currency dealings and over-night positions, low yen certificates of deposit limits, and Bank of Japan guidance to brokers affecting short term interest rates.

Energy. Half of the six energy-producing companies that participated in the survey said they were more restricted in Japan than in the US as to the goods and services they could provide.

Chemical–Pharmaceutical. The twenty-eight chemical, petro-chemical and pharmaceutical firms answering the questionnaire characterised Japan's product standards and product registration process as being, at times, 'nationalistic and subjective'. An unidentified manufacturer said he was faced with the following Catch-22: samples for registration purposes could not be imported until given registration approval, and registration approval could not be obtained until samples were analysed.

High technology. Government assistance and procurement practices posed problems for the eleven manufacturers of electronic components, data processing equipment, scientific instruments and computers who responded to the survey. A majority said government subsidies and assistance and government procurement practices discriminated against foreign firms.

Manufacturing. Manufacturers raised problems similar to those mentioned by chemical and pharmaceutical corporations. One firm noted as an example that US air-conditioning equipment could not be imported because the Japan 'High Pressure Vessel Code' required that equipment be inspected at the factory, but there were no Japanese inspectors in the US.

Insurance. Most of the US insurance companies agreed that the services they may offer were more restricted in Japan than in the US.

Publishing. Publishing companies complained of short-term (6 months) visas given to English-language translators, editors and teachers and that the Ministry of Justice limited the number of non-Japanese English speakers a company may sponsor.

Export/import. The twenty-five companies responding complained of product standards and the product registration process. Government procurement practices favored the Japanese, and customs regulations and procedures adversely affected their ability to do business were each noted by 32 per cent of the respondents.

Transportation. The two airlines responding criticised the preferential treatment given Japan Air Lines, and shipping firms complained of being prohibited from engaging in such affiliated services as trucking, warehousing and stevedoring. The shipping firms also noted that Japan Tobacco and Salt Public Corporation would not allow foreign carriers to ship American leaf tobacco to Japan.

In 1982 the Japanese government established an Office of Trade Ombudsman to handle complaints from foreign businessmen. At first businessmen were reluctant to use the Ombudsman because the name of the complainant had to be disclosed with the attendant risk of bureaucratic retaliation but this was partly overcome, in 1983, by allowing complaints to be submitted through proxies including foreign embassies. Numerous problems have been solved.

More recently, in October 1984, the European Business Council released a report on *Doing Business in Japan*. It 'recognized that there had been progress in the last few years where regulatory procedures in Japan once created obstacles to trade. But there are a number of areas where lack of harmonisation with international standards, and the refusal to accept foreign test data, create great difficulties for European exporters.' The report recommended changes in regulations and practice in the following areas:

(a) Pharmaceuticals. A satisfactory system whereby a company applying for the registration of a new drug is able to participate directly in the deliberation of the data by the Ministry's expert committees is requested. Faster evaluation of applications (currently averaging 2.5 years) is also called for. Recommendations also cover: 1. Revision in the test requirements for degradation products. 2. Harmonisation of Japanese standards with internationally accepted practices of preclinical testing and the clear and unambiguous publication of such standards. 3. An acceptance of foreign clinical test data in appropriate circumstances.

(b) Diagnostics and medical equipment. A recognition of the essential difference between pharmaceuticals and in vitro diagnostics, and acceptance of international scientific practices for the evaluation of diagnostics and medical equipment. This includes the acceptance of foreign data generated in conformity with those practices.

(c) Cosmetics. The introduction of a negative list of ingredients similar to those used in the EC and USA.

(d) Agro-chemicals. 1. Acceptance of toxicological data generated overseas according to OECD Good Laboratory Practice guidelines. 2. The introduction of a system for obtaining official guidance on test data requirements prior to starting tests and direct access to the relevant expert committees to explain and discuss results during the evaluation of registration applications.

(e) Food additives. The adoption of a positive list of those additives which are approved internationally.

(f) Electrical appliances. The full recognition and implementation of International Electro-technical Commission Standards and the simplification of procedures for authorising foreign testing organisations.

(g) Motor vehicles. An increase in the maximum number of vehicles covered by the Handling Procedure for Small Quantity Motor Vehicles to 1000.

Tariffs and quotas. Whilst noting that the tariff cuts of the last two years represent a 'significant improvement', the EBC points out that these have only a marginal impact on the competitive position of European goods. The cuts have only come at a time when the Japanese domestic manufacturers are so strong that they are in a position to dominate the market. Even now, however, high tariffs remain on a number of manufactured products which force them into uncompetitive price ranges. The paper recommends that there should be further reductions in tariffs on: certain agricultural products, alcoholic beverages, vegetable and fruit products, leather and furs, machinery and sporting goods. It is pointed out that quota liberalisations in the Second and Third Packages announced by the Japanese Government did not concern European exports. The paper urges that some quotas should be increased and certain market restrictions which affect European exports should be lifted.

Industrial and intellectual property rights. The proper protection of industrial and intellectual properties being of great importance to people doing business in Japan, the EBC expresses disappointment that the subject was not mentioned in the 5th Package when so much could be done to improve the present situation. Particular points are listed, including the need for action against counterfeiting, misleading labelling and indications of origin, and for increased legal protection for trade secrets and service marks.

Difficulties in registering patents are emphasised and concern is expressed that unauthorised dealers can sell consumer durables to customers who are often unaware that they will not be protected by makers warranties or agent service agreements.

Legal services. Since 1955 Japan has been effectively closed to foreign lawyers. The admission of non-Japanese to practices is now based solely on passing examinations which less than 3 per cent of Japanese nationals who take them actually pass. A number of obstacles are discussed which effectively prevent foreign lawyers from practising in Japan. Nichibenren, the national organisation to which all Japanese lawyers are required to belong and which has statutory disciplinary powers over them, is seen as a sole arbiter of the issue on the Japanese side. Proposals put forward by Nichibenren according to which foreign lawyers might be allowed to practise in Japan are described as 'restrictive'. The EBC feels that as business in Japan has become more international so a new area of demand has been created for experienced lawyers with international expertise. 'Legal consultants' could fulfil that role. They would not litigate in Japan but would rather provide legal advice both to Japanese companies requiring expertise on some aspect of foreign law and to foreign companies needing information about the situation in Japan seen from the perspective of their own national legal system.

Other recommendations covered Europe's investment in Japan, financial services and other sectors.

In November 1984 United States Secretary of State George Shultz said: 'On the whole, we believe that Japan's trade initiatives have improved foreign access to the Japanese market. It is clear, however, that significant barriers to trade still remain. Problems remain unsolved in almost all areas of bilateral trade, including telecommunications equipment, import tariffs, agricultural products, communications satellites, tobacco, services and investments.'

In 1986 the European Business Council of the European Community asked Japan to

eliminate tax and duty protectionism against imported bottled wines and spirits by:
1. Reducing import duties to the same level as the European Community.
2. Taxing spirits and liqueurs at a single specific rate pro rata to alcoholic content.

3. Taxing wines at a single specific rate pro rata to volume.

Japanese companies have, in post-war years, sought joint ventures to secure foreign technology but many of them, having mastered the technology and having been allowed to run the ventures fully, now feel that the joint ventures have become meaningless and a drag on building their own strength. Dissatisfaction has been expressed with 50:50 ventures as being inflexible because neither party had dominance. With the best of intentions from both sides, joint ventures encounter difficulties when market conditions change. During the 1974–5 oil crisis and subsequent yen–dollar exchange fluctuations, there have been many cases of joint ventures being terminated or of one partner buying full control.

In 1986 and 1987 overseas construction firms put up a mighty struggle, with their governments' help to participate in bidding for contracts for the building of the Osaka airport. Of equal significance, in 1987, has been the struggle by British and American firms to join a Japanese consortium being established to take over part of the functions of the earlier semi-government monopoly of international telecommunication services. The law allowed non-Japanese participants up to 33 per cent of the shareholding. The Japanese government struggled to keep this down and to divide it among a number of overseas organisations none of whom would have any share in management. Also in 1987, foreign lawyers still fought for the right to practise in Japan.

On the other hand, in 1987, America prevented a Japanese electronic company, Fujitsu, from purchasing a major American manufacturer, Fairchild Semiconductor Corporation. Also in 1987 the Reagan administration took the extreme action of threatening to increase import duties to 100 per cent on a very wide range of Japanese electronic goods entering the United States, on the ground that, after eight months, the Japanese government had failed to implement an agreement to limit the export of electronic chips.

This case list is of more than historic interest. It serves as an example of the myriad ways in which business outsiders have been treated by the Japanese clan. The Japanese government, criticised because of its gigantic trade surpluses, has pledged itself to open its market to the world. Much has been done to encourage imports but other countries are far from satisfied.

A constant problem for the alien businessman is that the interpretation of many Japanese laws is as important as their wording.

Regular liaison may be needed with the administration to know what is wanted. In this the Japanese businessmen have an advantage as they keep in constant touch with the bureaucrats.

Japan is not a closed market, but neither is it an open one.

17 Are the Japanese Efficient?

EFFICIENCY

It is a misconception in the West that, in all sectors of her economy, Japan is not just efficient, but superlatively and consistently so. Her huge trade surpluses in the mid-1980s pay tribute to her excellence in manufacturing and selling, but the success of the majority may conceal the failure of many.

Only rarely does a very large company go into liquidation. The major manufacturers are essentially assemblers of components supplied to them under rigid control by contractors who in their turn may employ sub-contractors who may rely on sub-sub-contractors. These smaller firms employ an overwhelming proportion of the total manufacturing work-force. They are the ones which go bankrupt when changes in demand affect the larger firm above them. From 1980–86 there was an average each year of over 15 000 bankruptcies, mainly in industry and trade, of companies each with debts of over ten million yen. In 1984 alone there were over 20 000 cases with combined liabilities of 3 640 000 million yen. Some economists may say that the bankruptcies of small firms are evidence of the efficiency of Japan's intensely competitive system, but the localised damage is noteworthy.

Of even greater significance are differences in efficiency between large sectors of the economy. Taking the standard yard-stick of labour productivity, Japan is super-efficient in some secondary (manufacturing) industries, but is backward in her primary (agriculture, fishing and forestry) and tertiary (distribution and service) industries.

Statistics are always dangerous tools. In comparing Japan with other countries they can be very misleading. Variations in currencies vitiate many comparisons. During the Allied Occupation after the Second World War (1945–52) and for the next 20 years one dollar was exchanged at a fixed, government-controlled exchange rate of 360 yen (and one sterling pound equalled 1008 yen). The value of the yen rose when decontrolled. Between October 1978 and

December 1982 it fluctuated between 176 and 278 yen to the dollar. In February 1985, after more violent fluctuations the exchange rate was 263. By March 1987 it was 146. Changes of such magnitude make many figures unrealistic. If, for instance, the average income of a Japanese was rated at 400 000 yen and the exchange rate 250 this translated into 1600 dollars, but if the exchange rate was 150 the dollar income became 2666. While the average Japanese worker was receiving the same yen income his 'standard of living' could be said to have grown enormously in comparison with the wages of his dollar-earning counterpart in America.

In addition to distortions to some statistics by wildly fluctuating exchange rates, the bases on which figures are calculated vary from country to country. For instance, when is a person who is not working classified as unemployed? Or, is labour productivity based on total labour output or on value added? Or, when is a machine a robot? The statistical methods used in compiling figures quoted here have not been minutely scrutinised. They are included as illustrations only and should be used with caution, particularly when comparing figures between countries. They do, however, give a basis for some generalisations.

A usual measure of efficiency between countries is to compare only manufacturing output per unit of labour. In this field the annual growth of productivity in Japan since 1945 when its factories were in ruins rose for about 30 years at a very much faster rate than in other countries. The rate of increase then slowed down and, on absolute figures, productivity at all times has been less impressive than the growth rate. Manufacturing, moreover, accounts for less than 30 per cent of Japan's gross national product and employs less than 35 per cent of her working population.

In 1987 the Japan Productivity Centre published an international comparison of value-added labour productivity levels (GDP per employee) for national economies in 1982: United States 131, Belgium 113, France 111, West Germany 109, Japan 100, Britain 80. The Japanese figure is unimpressive because this overall picture includes primary and tertiary production. For manufacturing only (excluding agriculture, construction, mining, electricity, gas, water, transport, storage, communication, financing, insurance, real estate and services) the figures are: United States 102, Japan 100, Belgium 94, France 93, West Germany 84 and Britain 56.

While the levels of value-added productivity in 1982 are important, the trends more significant from 1975 (100) to 1982 are even. The

Japan Productivity Centre figures for national economies are: Japan 133, West Germany 120, Belgium 119, France 117 (1981), Britain 115, and the United States 104. For manufacturing only the comparative trends are Japan 177, Belgium 146, France 126 (1981), West Germany 122, Britain 115 and the United States 111.

Agriculture, fishing and forestry have fallen far behind manufacturing as a source of Japan's wealth. Although they remain an important part of the economy, workers engaged in the primary industries have dropped from about 50 per cent to about 3 per cent of the working population in the last 50 years. In this primary sector value-added productivity in 1982 compared unfavourably with that in other industrialised countries: Belgium 513, United States 434, Britain 396, France 244 (1981), West Germany 221, Japan 100. (The trend of agricultural value-added productivity in Japan from 1975 to 1982 lagged far behind that of the other five countries. Japan Productivity Centre figures.)

The retail prices of some of Japan's agricultural products have been boosted to protect a small segment of the community at the expense of the nation's consumers. To keep the farmers' and city workers' standards of living about the same, and to hold the important farmers' vote for the ruling political party, the government buys the nation's entire rice crop and sells it at a slightly lower price. Until recently distribution was restricted to licenced dealers to sell through the stores they had used for generations. There has been change. Supermarkets and local grocery shops may now sell rice.

Farmers, finding rice growing more profitable than other crops, have produced more and more. Annual production is about ten million tons. Wheat products are cheaper. Rice consumption has fallen by about 40 per cent from the 118 kilograms per person eaten in 1952. Since 1967 production has greatly exceeded consumption every year except one year with abnormal weather (1984). Most years there have been huge surplus stocks.

In 1970 government expenditure for agriculture reached about ten trillion yen, about 8 per cent of its whole budget. The government had to restrict the rice-growing acreage and pay subsidies to leave part of the land untilled. The surplus, perishable stock (over six million tons in 1982) has been sold at prices about one third of the consumer's price, for 'non-staple food purposes'. By 1987 the cost to the taxpayer was reduced to about 400 billion yen, about 0.7 per cent of the budget.

Surplus stocks have not been exported. The price is too high. The general public pays treble world prices and, as taxpayers, carries a heavy additional burden. It seems, however, to be reluctant to press the government to permit import of cheap rice in spite of pressure from Japan's trading partners to open the Japanese market. It is widely believed that rice from other countries is not as tasty as Japanese-produced rice.

Distribution and services also play a large part in reducing Japan's overall productivity. International value-added labour productivity in 1982 for commerce and services was: United States 140, France 125 (1981), West Germany 124, Belgium 110, Japan 100, Britain 78 (Japan Productivity Centre figures). These tertiary industries have grown to absorb more than half the country's employed workers (56.9 per cent in 1983 compared with 29.2 per cent engaged in manufacturing). By one economist's definition, Japan has thus passed the test that she is a 'developed' country, but her over-staffed distribution and service channels are notoriously complicated by conventions and regulations which maintain human relations in a seriously inefficient system. To protect what are, in effect, cottage industries in the form of small, family-run retail shops, the government has put obstacles in the way of the expansion of large department stores, supermarkets and chain stores.

> Manufacturers sell through a complex multi-stage wholesale structure, using many intermediaries and retail outlets. (Although this adds to distribution costs, it also shows in practice a keenly competitive side of Japan's communal system.) Since the first oil shock in 1973, much has been done to streamline distribution, but there remains room for more developments to make the services sector of the economy efficient.

The domestic market has been neglected. Housing is riddled with restrictive practices and archaic land and rental policies. Japan must be one of the few countries in the world where owners never display 'For Sale' signs on their properties. A reduction in housing costs could produce a new lead sector for the economy in spite of the unreasonably high price of land.

The consumers are demanding and require elaborate packing which creates waste on an enormous scale. (My family wages a frustrating war to prevent shop assistants wrapping the goods we buy in unnecessary paper and packing them in unnecessary containers. Apart from the time it takes to unwrap in the home and to dispose of the superfluous coverings, the sheer waste is appalling.)

Vast sums are spent on advertising and entertainment. Business spent more or a similar amount on entertainment – 3 523 000 million yen for the year (or 9652 million yen each day) in 1983 – than the government spent on defence, or education or science. Companies pay more for entertainment than for dividends.

These negative comments on inefficiency in agriculture and the service industries and even in manufacturing, taken by themselves, are as misleading as the other extreme view that Japan is super-efficient in all fields. I have mentioned them to maintain perspective, Japan's efficiency in some manufacturing fields, particularly steel, electronics and automobile production, deserves full credit.

It is a commonly accepted myth that a country deficient in natural resources is at a great disadvantage against countries rich in the products. The facts point in the opposite direction. With the world as a single economic unit, countries are most efficient when they are able to import from the cheapest source. If a country has good ports and heavy industry located near them, ocean freight is a small factor when assessing costs. Japan's steel industry deserves high praise for its efficiency, but its reliance on imported iron ore and fuels has been no handicap to its shore-based mills.

Japan gains because it has to import almost all of its cotton, wool, bauxite, nickel, corn, crude oil, iron ore, tin and wheat. Even since the traumatic increases in world oil prices Japan, as it does not have to think of domestic producers, has been able to buy competitively. The United States had to raise oil prices to protect its domestic producers. The inefficiencies of Japan's economy are in areas where she insulates herself from world markets.

Efficient labour and Total Quality Control have been supplemented by the use of the most modern and technologically-advanced machinery and production methods concentrated on a narrow range of products with long production runs, and the vigorous promotion of sales abroad by thorough market research and energetic marketing. The giant trading companies have bought and sold at the best prices and welded industries which have concentrated on their prime function of manufacturing. A high growth-rate has avoided many restructuring difficulties. Close links between commerce, industry, the civil service and politicians have played their part.

Japan's stupendous achievements have created an enduring manu-facturing edifice during this last generation. She had invested hugely in production facilities. She is now an economic centre of the world with excellent capability in processing, manufacturing and assembling. Without worker opposition, Japan is leading the world in the revolutionary development and use of robots (although statistics can be misleading as some machinery is classified as 'robot' in Japan, but not in other countries). She has shown exceptional ability to benefit from an expanding world market. It is equally possible that she can adjust to a contracting one. Japan's economy is an integral part of the world, is geared to it, and dependent on it.

Japanese industry spends huge sums on research and development. According to OECD statistics Japan's private sector invested about 4 800 000 million yen in 1983. This, at the exchange rate at the time, was only about 30 per cent of the corresponding outlay in the United States but it was substantially more than the total amount spent in each European country. This expenditure was much heavier on development and applied than on basic research. For example, in 1984, the breakdown for the steel industry was: development research 127 583 million yen; applied research 51 295 million yen; basic research 13 214 million yen; total 192 091 million yen (Iron and Steel Federation figures). With the yen appreciation in 1986 and 1987, Japanese industry did not reduce its spending on research and development, but cut back heavily its annual investment in new equipment. (It speculated with its surplus funds on the share market and it is said that many companies made more money from these financial transactions in these years, than from their regular business.)

In passing it should be noted that Japan has made very efficient use of its financial resources, but the economy has had to lean heavily on the government. As recently as the end of 1985 the Japanese national government debt was 165 384 000 million yen or about 50 per cent of the 1985 gross national product. This was, on a per capita basis, about the same level as the United States' Federal debt. Japan's national debt is, however, mainly held by 'stable' investors in long-term bonds with maturities of 10 or 20 years, whereas the US Treasury debt is largely in comparatively short-term bills and notes. Since 1985 Japan's relative position has greatly improved, but her national debt is far from being insignificant.

While the West has much to learn from Japan, a brief reminder is advisable. Japanese managements work through consensus and are not always efficient. They also may learn from the West.

In Japan the chief executives spend much of their time in purely formal ceremonials and conferences. The Western director has more time to devote to deciding broad policy and to streamlining his organisation.

Western organisations employ non-executive directors from other spheres and do not discourage their senior executives from taking seats on other Boards. The Japanese are reluctant to admit to their inner circles outsiders who are not their totally committed intimates. Even a small widening of contacts and breaking down of barriers at the top level of management might lead to broader developments.

The Western business leader is personally and promptly accountable for his company's results, good or bad. His business must make a profit. If it fails he has no excuse and a top manager can be replaced before his company drifts downwards too far. Japanese managers may also be retired, but rarely before the company's finances have become so strained that creditors are compelled to step in.

As innovators, small manufacturing units, which are more independent and common in the West and which are more autocratically governed by a single man at the head, may be as effective as the research laboratories of very large companies.

The Japanese are accustomed to consensus decisions with all the delays and rigidities this involves, whereas Western management derives some advantages from dispute, rivalry and conflict.

Neither system is perfect and there is no doubt that Japan is very efficient in many ways.

18 The Economic Scene

TODAY

Japan's industrial and commercial successes are constantly praised in newspapers, magazines and books published around the world. Similar compliments are paid indirectly by her trading partners when they complain of her export goods 'dumped' at low prices with disastrous damage to manufacturers in the importing countries. They also growl that Japan's domestic market is not open for the import of their goods, and point out that any expansion would benefit Japan as well as the rest of the world. In 1987 a further opening of Japan's market was still being demanded by America and the European Community.

The Japanese attitude towards outsiders has not changed. Her huge surplus of exports over imports year by year and her growing investments in overseas countries testify to her competitive and expanding commercial power. There are solid reasons for the world to applaud and complain.

On 24 March 1987 the *Japan Times*, the leading English language daily newspaper, held an International Symposium to celebrate its ninetieth birthday. A small number of distinguished Japanese and foreigners were invited to speak on 'Can Japan Become an International Power?' The British Ambassador, Sir John Whitehead, outlined changes in Japan during the last 30 years in the following words:

In Japanese terms anyone who is 90 years old is worthy of considerable respect as a person with long experience and sound judgment which comes from having reached somewhat late middle age! And so it is with the *Japan Times*. A paper founded in Meiji times at the end of the nineteenth century, less than 30 years after the Meiji Restoration, it has experienced much – the Russo-Japanese war and the Treaty of Portsmouth, the Anglo-Japanese naval alliance, the world depression of the 1920s, the troubles of the 1930s, the world war of the 1940s followed by the occupation, the San Francisco Peace Treaty and the rebuilding of Japan to a major position of prominence in the world in the 1980s. It is amazing that there has been one Emperor of Japan for two-thirds of that time, a changing continuity in an age of substantial discontinuity.

I have been a reader of the *Japan Times*, on and off, for 31 years, just over a third of its existence. The first editions I read in Japan were for 15 and 16 November 1956. Looking at them again I am amazed at the similarity of the format with that of today's editions. Since those days Japanese policies, whether they be commercial, economic, financial, foreign or defence, have developed substantially. The passing of time has been marked by practical developments: In 1956 the *Japan Times* cost Y10, in 1987 Y140. In 1956 the paper noted that there were 300 000 TV sets in Japan; more than half were in Tokyo, there were 76 000 in Osaka, 36 000 in Nagoya and 5 300 in Sendai. A 3-bedroom house in Azabu with a spacious garden was advertised for Y65 000 a month. (Rentals in 1987 have risen to as much as Y2 000 000 a month.) In those days we were still 8 years away from the Tokyo Olympics; taxis came in 2 sizes: a Datsun at Y60 and a Toyopet at Y70, (now the meter starts at Y470); there were trams on the streets down Aoyama-dori and Uchibori-dori, cobbles on the roads, only one short subway line from Shibuya to Ginza, Marunouchi was redbrick, much of the housing in central Tokyo was made of wood, and it was still to be some years before the Kasumigaseki building with its 36 stories was opened as the tallest building in Asia.

It was a time when the textile industry in Japan was in its heyday and when Japanese foreign policy consisted of the payment of reparations following the war, the search for raw materials to fuel Japanese industry which was then rapidly being rebuilt, and the solution of individual problems such as fishing negotiations with the Americans, Canadians or Russians, difficulties with Korea over Japanese boats which strayed across the Rhee Line, and the repatriation of Japanese from Siberia and other places. There was a Security Treaty with the United States; there were rudimentary Self Defence Forces. It was a period when Japan was immensely inward-looking; its relations with countries in this region, let alone elsewhere, were limited and somewhat uneasy.

Twelve years later, by the end of the 60s, Japanese industry had become one of the most dynamic in the world, real rates of growth each year were in double figures, the steel industry had a capacity of 160 million tons, Japanese shipyards were taking more than half of the world's orders, Japanese cars and electrical goods were being shipped all over the world. Japanese foreign policy was more developed but still rather tentative, with large areas of the world with which Japan had commercial but no real political relations. Japanese defence policy continued to lag behind in its development. It was at the end of the 1960s that Japan and the United States had their first major difficult trade negotiation – on textiles – which was to herald a whole series of trade-friction problems which have lasted until now. The trade problems with some countries in Western Europe were also becoming a persistent feature of relations with that part of the world.

The 1970s were marked by the two oil shocks, the normalisation of relations with China, the drastic restructuring of the Japanese shipbuilding and shipping industries and the maturing of Japanese industry with GNP growth rates down to an average of about 5 per cent. The Japanese balance of payments went into the black and other countries clamoured for greater access to a market which had been kept remarkably closed but which now had a great deal of purchasing power. The two main lines of Japanese foreign policy, one across the Pacific to North America and the other down the Eastern seaboard of Asia, had been strengthened but also diversified. Japan was taking a closer interest in the Indian Ocean, the Middle East, Europe and East–West relations.

The 1980s with further maturing of the economy, the still lower growth rates of 3 per cent or so, the move up-market into high-tech industries and into invisibles, particularly financial services and overseas investment, in marketing capacity as well as securities, is part of very recent history. So is, I suggest, the final establishment of a worldwide conceptualised Japanese foreign policy, perhaps the last element of which is the much greater political as well as economic interest which Japan is now taking in Southern Africa.

It is tempting to close this book with Sir John's excellent outline of Japan's recent past (together with his words of wisdom of p. 187). However, a few words relating to the quality of Japanese people's lives may be added.

In the last 30 years high-rise modern edifices have mushroomed, literally from the ashes of flimsy, single-storied wooden buildings; new underground railways have been burrowed to an extent that would amaze the most sophisticated of rabbits; trains are faster and more frequent though hardly less jampacked; roads have been surfaced, a few widened and some new ones built; television, refrigeration and Western heating, clothing and foods make significant contributions to Japanese life. At first glance it seems that, as the nation has prospered in its international trade, the Japanese people must have also.

However, speculative and ridiculous increases in city and suburban land prices have benefited a few at the cost of many. The average Japanese worker dreams of a house he may never be able to buy. The overcrowding of the cities has put a great strain on public and private transport. Trains and buses are intolerably crowded. A majority of city workers stand for more than an hour each working day, morning and evening, each way between home and office. Japan suffers from more cars to the mile of road than any other industrialised country. Water supply and sewerage services are inadequate.

The cost of education is extremely high. Just one item was the average cost of admission only to a university (other than the few national ones). It averaged 970 000 yen for each student in 1987. Welfare services do not give adequate security to the majority of the people. Consumers pay excessively high prices for their food to protect the farmers. An example of the high cost of living is that wedding ceremonies are unbelievably expensive.

A 1984 bank survey reported that, for the average couple, marriage related costs were 6.86 million yen of which the bridegroom's side met 2.93 and the bride's 3.93. A breakdown of these sums gives some insights into the workings of Japanese society. The bridegroom's expenses were: betrothal gifts to the bride's parents 840 000; furniture and home expenses 1 380 000; the wedding ceremony and party 430 000; and the honeymoon 280 000. On the bride's side: 420 000 to the parents of the groom; 2 800 000 for furniture and and the home; 430 000 for the ceremony and party; and for the honeymoon 280 000. It was also found that the average couple invited to the ceremony and party 84 relatives and friends who, on the average, gave 13 000 yen as a wedding gift. Minus the cash gifts from relatives and friends the balance of wedding related expenditures was 1 950 000 for the groom and 2 530 000 for the bride. The total spent on marriages throughout the land is said to be about 4 000 000 000 yen per year, about 8 per cent of the national budget.

Pollution has taken its toll, not just in the extreme cases of the suffering and lives of those poisoned to disability or death by mercury and cadmium from the factories but also in the deterioration of health of those who inhale too much of the noxious gases emitted by factories and cars (CO).

Good agricultural land and forests have been diminished to make way for industries and the population concentrated around them. Cumulative environmental destruction continues. Little has been done to prevent the trend or to restore the damage. Japan's urban population, concentrated in a narrow strip of the country from Tokyo to Kobe, suffers from a lack of parks in its cities, the devastation of much of the adjoining countryside and the abandonment of the more remote.

This mixture of adverse factors shows that the Japanese economic structure, like all others, is not perfect. There is some validity in the thought that the Japanese have deprived themselves as persons to ensure that their nation has prospered. Some cynics say of Japan, 'Rich nation, poor people' but, carried to this extreme, they could extend their devastating catch-phrase to cover every nation in the world by listing the negative factors in each. If we name only unemployment, inflation and the possibility of nuclear war there are no 'Rich nations, rich people'.

The less than favourable factors are only part of the picture of the living conditions of the people. There is also a bright side which is often taken for granted. Wages are high in cash terms (making Japan internationally uncompetitive in labour-intensive industries) and the Japanese people are now well supplied with many amenities: coloured television sets, radios, washing machines, refrigerators, cars, air-conditioners. The packaging, delivery and aftersale service, which includes the acceptance back of goods for the flimsiest of reasons, are magnificent within stereotyped limitations. Delivery of meals to the home is widely available. Consumers require, and are given, service no longer available in other lands. The quality of life in Japan has risen dramatically in the last three decades.

TOMORROW

Has Japan risen to a pinnacle, or reached a plateau, or a precipice? Will she fall back or rise further? There are negative and positive spots in her economy which should not be overlooked.

An outstanding feature of living and doing business in Japan and with Japan is that one is never certain what is going to happen at any hour of every day. The Japanese day-to-day interpretation of the domestic scene and of events in other countries play havoc with established business routines and actions. The present is crammed with the unexpected. The future is even more unpredictable. However, an understanding of the culture acts as a shock absorber and some events are clear with the benefit of hindsight.

Much that helped Japan surge forward from the time of the Korean War no longer exists. That war gave Japan an unlimited world market and American finance to rebuild her shattered factories, but it lasted for only a few years. The support given by the USA to help Japan to rise from poverty to wealth has now been moderated. Instead of being an ailing ally Japan is now expected to pull her weight on equal terms. This is particularly noticeable in the military sphere. For years Japan managed to keep her military expenditure at a low level. Now the costs of her Self Defence Forces are becoming a significant part of her annual budget although her little over 1 per cent of GNP is still negligible when compared with the United States' budget for defence.

Overall growth has continued at a solid level in spite of 'oil shocks', fluctuating exchange rates and competition from neighbouring nations who have been advancing their industrialisation with the advantages of low paid work-forces such as Japan had made the most of in earlier decades. Recessions have not crippled Japan's major industries. Some have declined or changed their main product lines. New ones have sprung up. Depressions have hurt small corporations, but large businesses have sailed through the post-war storms.

Labour is no longer as plentiful in Japan as it was. Unemployment, in comparison with other industrialised countries, is low, but far from negligible. In 1987 it had risen to about 3 per cent, even by Japanese definition, but, at the same time, there were acute shortages in some industries – construction, electronics, computers. The unemployed were mostly of advanced age, or their training had not fitted them for the skills needed by the expanding industries. A shortage of labour by the year 2000 is predicted by some industrialists and economists. The average age of the labour force which was remarkably low is now much older. The ageing population becomes a more expensive source of labour, but women are playing a larger role and have the potential to make a much greater contribution. Some highly efficient industries are now geared to large-scale, automated production of high quality goods and have reduced their

vulnerability to a shortage of labour and to competition from the
cheap goods from low-wage countries.

There is not now the desperate need to work hard or to go without
the necessities of life, but most Japanese still realise that to consume
one should produce. The security of 'lifetime' employment and the
annual wage increases which were standard are no longer universal.
Real wages have trebled, but the cost of living has increased. The
Japanese live in small houses which, even when located far from
city centres, are much more expensive than larger ones in the West.
Though they have learned to use cramped quarters very effectively,
they no longer accept with equanimity the 'matchbox' houses to
which they are heir. The Japanese are still industrious though signs
of the lethargy of affluence, the European malady, are to be seen
and disturb some commentators.

This recitation of facts is to remind us that although Japan's
growth has amazed the world, and is continuing at more moderate
speed, all is never perfect. There are many indications of her strength
and potential. Her success still comes largely from maintaining low
interest rates in a world in which most countries have allowed high
interest to cripple their industries and inflation to weaken their
economies. Japanese industry makes profits year by year. Dividends
have been kept low and profits ploughed back into new equipment,
research work and other ways that will increase profits in the years
to come. This has been going on for so many years that her industrial
strength has become solid. Of great significance, Japan is investing
her surplus funds overseas in the way that advanced European
countries and America did during their periods of growth. Japan
has become the largest creditor nation in the world, outstripping the
USA and Britain. Japan's net external assets grow rapidly. Receiving
income from other countries instead of having to pay makes for a
sound economy. Money makes money.

To predict Japan's future a book could be devoted to her economic
prospects. One could weigh the strength of her present huge
favourable trade balances, and growing investments overseas against
her domestic public debt and budget deficits – persisting deficits
which, before the United States took its recent deficit course,
reached almost the combined total of those of the United States,
Britain, Germany and France. Japan is part of the world economy,
at the mercy of booms and depressions over which she has little
control. Until very recently undervaluation of the yen, with its
distortions of world trade, came from unrealistic US interest and

exchange rates. World commerce has a tremendous impact, the productivity of Japan's labour, her GNP, her savings habits, the quality of life, her ageing population and a host of other factors should be watched to gauge how she will weather storms not of her making.

The government Economic Planning Agency is remarkably optimistic. Its forecasts made public on 26 March 1987 show a Japanese view of the future. It estimated that Japan would overtake the United States in per capita gross national product in 1993 when Japan's per capita GNP would come to $22 000 compared with $19 000 it forecasted for the United States. The report added that Japan's net credits would balloon from the current $130 000 million to $730 000 million in 1993 while the United States accumulated current account deficits would increase eleven-fold to $1 200 000 million. In 1993 Japan would account for 13.4 per cent of the world's total GNP compared with its 1986 11.8 per cent according to the report which assumed a real annual growth rate of an average 4 per cent for Japan and 2.2 per cent for the United States. The report added that Japan's overseas investments would increase by 1993 to $370 000 million compared to those of West Germany, Britain, France and Italy which would combine to $490 000! These prognostications will no doubt be changed long before 1993 and one hopes that Japan will broaden her goals from her own prosperity to include humanitarian ends and, in her own interests, to recycling and restructuring the debt position of developing countries.

After this optimistic Japanese prediction, it is fitting to round off with Sir John Whitehead's comments at the 1987 *Japan Times* symposium. He said:

I have spelt out a potted, and very impressionistic, history of the emergence of Japan on the world stage over the last 30 years as a major player for several reasons. First, because I think it is important for us to recognise how rapid that emergence has been – even though in certain aspects some of the moves have seemed to others to be excruciatingly slow. Second, because I think it is also important for us to recognise how short some of the individual industrial cycles, which have been such a factor not only for Japan's internal development but also of her relations with other countries, are. The *Japan Times* of 16 November 1956 to which I referred earlier contained a special section on the Japanese textile industry headed: 'Woollen Exports Zoom as Industry

Completes Postwar Rehabilitation'. It was just 12 years later that the difficult Japan/US textile negotiations started; and it was not much more than 12 years after that that large parts of the textile industry had been restructured or ceased to exist as a result of other countries with lower unit costs moving into positions formerly occupied by Japan. The Y60 Datsun cars of 1956 had by 1970 become, under the guidance of Mr Ishihara and others at Nissan, some of the best-known cars in the world, which led to certain problems and subsequently in the 1980s to the welcome investment by Nissan in North East England (as well as investment in other parts of the world). The 160 million tons of steel capacity of the 1960s was never fully utilised and production is now something like 90 million tons and falling. In shipbuilding, Korea has pretty well caught up with Japan because of the very substantial difference in unit costs.

Third, and perhaps most importantly, no country which has an economy of any strength can nowadays be an island. The economics of the developed countries (and the developing economies too) are remarkably closely linked. A country can protect its industry for just so long before irresistible pressure builds up. A country's currency can be undervalued for a while, but in recent years with floating exchange rates, highly developed foreign exchange markets, rapid communications systems and moves towards the relaxation or abolition of exchange controls, a currency rapidly reflects the underlying strength or otherwise of an economy, almost whatever happens to interest rates.

Fourth, in a much closer-knit world, economic strength brings with it political problems, opportunities and responsibilities. Given her constitution, this is an area in which Japan has stated that her role will be played substantially through the medium of financial and technical assistance. But Japan's interest in for example the progress of East/West exchanges about Intermediate Range Nuclear Weapons and her concern about the stationing of SS-20s in Siberia show the extent to which one is inevitably affected by politico-military developments as well.

In these circumstances, you may well ask, why has the question been posed of whether Japan can become an international power? Surely with a 10 per cent share of all the goods and services produced in the world, with developed markets in virtually every single country in the world, with one of the strongest currencies in the world and with Tokyo being – along with London and New

York – one of the three financial centres of the world, with a developed foreign policy and a major assistance programme, Japan is already without any doubt a major power on the international scene? Yes, but ...

And part of the 'but' was discussed in an article by Professor Yoshida of Kyoto University which originally appeared in the Sankei Shimbun and was reproduced in the *Japan Times* a few days ago. I found it thought-provoking even though I could not say that I agreed with it all. I came to the conclusion, not for the first time, that much depended on one's standpoint and interests and that remarkably little is or can be judged entirely objectively. He concluded that 'Westerners attach a seemingly unchanging value to their own tradition. It is precisely this constancy of values which we lack. Japanese live their lives within a framework of constantly altering values. Amid this cultural uncertainty, the Japanese people are now actually shifting the very axis of their own civilisation.' I wonder. Professor Yoshida seems to regret the shift to some Japanese industrial production overseas and goes on to warn that internationalisation 'only results in Japanese who can more or less cope with the cultural order of another society. Do not look for any profound transcendental synthesis of Japanese and foreign values. It is not going to happen.' In my view, more is the pity.

Surely what we are looking for is indeed much more interchange (if not exactly a synthesis of values) in almost all fields, cultural and otherwise. The West, broadly termed, has indeed had changing values: many of the countries of Western Europe have embarked, in forming a European Community, on perhaps one of the greatest historical voyages of all time. There are innumerable difficulties and frustrations along the way, but many of our historical and traditional ways of looking at things are gradually changing. It is a cooperative as well as inevitably at times a confrontational process. It involves countries with 300 million people, with a generally high standard of living, resourceful, inventive, with long historical links with almost every part of the world. One has to be a Euro-pessimist not to feel at least periodic excitement at this development when viewed in a broad historical perspective.

And yet, dare one say it, there is a tendency in this part of the world repeatedly to adopt two attitudes: to assert that the 21st century will be the century of the Pacific Basin and to ignore

Europe or write it off. Yes, Japan is a major power on the international scene; yes, Japan can become an international power in the sense that I believe was meant by those who posed the question for this seminar. But we must still look for many more Japanese to travel overseas and gain experience of other countries and cultures; and we must also look for a less closed cultural approach to good ideas, influences and products of a wide variety from overseas. At present there still remains in many aspects of Japanese life an attitude that change will affect the integrity of Japanese society and culture and that it should only come about to a minimal and highly controlled extent and then only in response to foreign pressure. To become a truly international power I think that this (to a foreigner) rather cramped and over-protective stance must shift much further than it has so far in the years to come.

19 Japan's Competitive-Communism

Western civilisation has reached its present level through the drive of individuals. The Japanese, in obtaining industrial results the envy of other nations, have shown that communal dependence on the collective will is also capable of very effective twentieth-century achievement. Intimate human relations and group dependence in all aspects of social life, unchanged over a thousand years, and leavened at all levels with competition and the profit incentive, has accommodated itself successfully to modern situations. Japan has long experience in restraining individualism, achieving harmony by compromise, settling conflicts between insiders, and overcoming conflicts with outsiders. Consensus decision making and all aspects of labour relations are even more communal, i.e. communistic, than in countries recognised to be communist. In trade, industry and commerce motivation is spurred by the hope for financial gain and, for the individual, ego may also be inflated by raised status.

Large and small cliques (the clan, fraternities and cells) give a communal framework to Japanese society. Japanese fraternities, ruled from within, compete fiercely against one another, but also act together when they have a common interest. The communal, strict bureaucratic control yet competitive management of Japan's industrial resources, geared to make profits, opposes and at the same time goes hand-in-glove with government restraints and encouragements. But a great weakness of the clique system is the sharp divisions it creates between insiders and outsiders.

Close person-to-person relations and the cliques that have evolved play a major role in eliminating the broad upper, middle and lower class distinctions which are accepted in Europe and exist less obviously in America. In Japan grades substitute for class divisions and movement between grades is possible in practice as well as in theory. Changes in status through ability and educational qualifications in each generation cut against broader stratifications. In Japan rank within well-defined, implicitly accepted hierarchies combines with the reliance of seniors on juniors.

There is little nationalisation of industry. As in other capitalist countries, individuals, restricted only by their income, not state-control, may own every type of property including land, buildings, bonds and shareholdings in industry. The propensity to save makes a very large part of the population minor capitalists. Property owners may obtain 'unearned' income from their possessions and may pass their rights on to others. Nevertheless, even though individual Japanese may invest their capital in industry and obtain income from it, they have little influence over the management and policies of the companies in which they have invested. The holders of shares in commercial and industrial corporations are treated as unimportant outsiders not as capitalists who own the corporations. Most profits are retained for the benefit of the company, not distributed to the shareholders. Control is in the hands of senior employees who have risen to be the corporations' directors and who manage 'their' organisations immune from shareholders' wishes. The Japanese company is a community of workers, managers and directors with similar interests. Every company is very aware that, in a competitive economy, its success depends on selling its products and that the consumer has overriding power.

The bureaucratic organisation of large-scale industry, with 'lifetime' employment its hallmark, reflects communist ideals, but the Japanese approach to social living, despite its bureaucratic framework, does not accept the dictatorial controls of countries with communist government. The press is as free as in Western democracies. Secret police are not in evidence and there are no reports of unlawful arrest or torture of political prisoners. Japan displays an open parliamentary system without overt control of voting, but there are few signs that the public is sufficiently actively interested in politics to contribute as individuals to the election of members of the Diet. The Communist Party is not banned and anyone may vote for its candidates, but it has negligible power in the elected legislature.

The Western industrial system has for generations treated workers as wage-slaves who can be discarded at short notice. In post-war Japan industries have accepted more responsibility for their employees and the employees have seen the advantage to themselves of preserving the industries for which they work. Japan has become an industrial country without creating an antagonistic working class through centuries of conflict. She has developed a system which tends to select her ablest people to play important roles. The workers accept collective dominance within their cliques which they have little freedom of choice to join or leave. Japan has shown that her system works in today's world and has not yet had to change to accept the individualism of the West. If the world is moving away from small-scale private enterprise towards a bureaucratically administered society then Japan leads the world. However, will her competitive-communism continue?

The part played by machinery in the social system is not confined to its significance when comparing the productivity of labour between countries. When considering the Japan of tomorrow the growing use of automation and computers could have unexpected results. The present communal dependence that comes from cliques of people working closely together may be diluted as the organisation of teamwork is displaced by single workers responsible for the control of masses of complicated machinery. The social organisation will remain vital although its functioning may require significant adjustments.

Firms are reducing the priority that has been placed on years of employment with the company and now relate the individual's wages more to his, or her, ability. This may diminish loyalty to corporations and dependence on the communal system. The growing number of workers who change their positions shows that the Japanese worker has the same desires as the Western worker if a choice of jobs is open. Influenced by the world outside, the Japanese post-war generation accepts the confines of the old system less wholeheartedly than its seniors. The new generation may lessen the pace of the treadmill their elder work-mates keep turning. Greater mobility of labour, and with it the growth of individualism, will follow if job opportunities exceed the supply of labour. This situation has not been reached but it may before the end of the 1990s.

There has been a marked increase in the number of men and women who show individuality and divorce themselves from the conformity of the group. Nowadays an amazing number of Japanese travel abroad alone, breaking completely from the communal domination at home. However, with the dramatic increase of twenty years in the average Japanese life expectancy, a higher proportion of senior citizens in the population may support existing systems, and increasing employment of women and of those beyond the presently low retirement age levels, their wages reduced, add to the supply of cheap labour. A shortage of jobs inhibits change.

More environmental and technological developments there will be, of course, but a switch from deeply embedded dependence on cliques and harmony to belief in personal freedom of choice could generate traumatic psychological and social repercussions. In spite of the spectacular environmental developments, longstanding person-to-person dependence has so far remained remarkably stable. Significant change is obstructed by language, childhood training, custom, inertia and the success of the present communistic social structure.

Despite the wholesale adoption and adaption of foreign words, the Japanese language remains majestically impervious to basic modification. Non-verbal communication plays a significant role though it does not function well in large communities. The language remains vague with overtones emphasising the rank of those engaged in a dialogue. In Japan substantial change is unlikely until the language is revised fundamentally.

Of the forces which resist change dependency, fostered from birth by childhood training, stands as a sign of continuity. The system is perpetuated by the Japanese mother when she teaches her child to rely on her, not to become a separate person hardened to fight life's battles on his, or her, own feet. Highly developed feelings of dependence and belongingness, implanted by this childhood training and expanded into adult life, are the continuing mainsprings of Japanese behaviour.

A growing number of mothers are leaving their children to strangers during the day while they work. As more crèches are opened and outside baby-sitters replace mothers and mothers-in-law, so will the baby's total reliance on its mother and family diminish. Many new brides refuse to live with parents-in-law. As nuclear families proliferate and more and more live in 'modern' blocks of flats, the family hierarchy is being challenged. Against all this, there are scholars who believe that the child's dependence is moulded in its first three months of constant maternal presence. Mothers now have more time to devote to their small families and most keep their children dependent on them even though they do not carry their babies on their backs as frequently as in the past.

As yet there is little evidence of a majority, or even a sufficiently powerful minority, strongly enough motivated to alter the social structure. There are, however, many young people resisting the system and there are many indications that things may not remain as they are. The seeds of change have been planted and the soil is fertile. The growing time is anyone's guess.

If the Japanese have a lesson to learn as well as to teach, it is that people can remain distinctive and proud of their culture without isolating themselves and their nation. For Japan to continue to think and act with narrow, selfish economic aims, ignoring her wider interests in the way one of her provincial domains tried to remain independent of its nation a hundred years ago, could be tragic. Japan's nationalism may be enhanced if she shifts her sights from national aggrandisement to taking a leading role in the family of nations for international and, hence, national achievement. As a step in this direction clan solidarity will have to relax its exclusiveness and rigidities towards outsiders.

The Japanese have become so expert in the arts of practical compromise to achieve consensus and harmony that, when they see the advantages to their clan of working constructively with other nations, they could play a leading role in world management. As the Japanese always expect change, they are psychologically conditioned to accept it. Their ability to co-operate or compete depending on the immediate situation can give them advantages in negotiations.

It is, to the Western mind, a weakness that Japan does not have rigid basic standards on which to build specific policies and to remain with her decisions. To expect this is to ignore the Japanese emotional, situational approach to immediate problems. They are reluctant to accept defined policies which cannot easily be switched when circumstances change. Japanese yardsticks are at total variance from those of the West. Rationality and logic have long been thought, in the West, to be principal elements in modern industrialised societies. Western logic, reasoning and rationality which stem from debate have yet done little more than dent Japan's traditional culture. The Japanese have proved that concentration on the tangible, immediate situation also produces the most sophisticated economic growth. Even though discussion that ignores logic can be a stumbling block to communication, the West may exaggerate the advantages of abstract standards and of putting everything into perspective. We Westerners should not forsake the tyranny of reason but, at the same time, we may learn from the Japanese example to concern ourselves more with the immediate and the practical. The future world does not have to cling to Western methods unchanged. Neither does Japan have to hold inflexibly to her traditional characteristics.

The West has learned from centuries of international conflict the necessity of mutual concessions. It should be able to compromise with Japan's contradictory and versatile actions that arise inevitably from her almost total reliance on human relations and communal pressures. Transplanting cultures as a whole is impractical, but the Japanese expertise in assimilating from others leaves no doubt that partial adaptions carefully tailored to their new environments may benefit the recipients. The West could assimilate part of Japan's system by developing greater co-operation between managements and workers.

Despite her high standing in today's world, Japan cannot close her doors and live independently. She depends on imports and exports for her lifeblood. Trade friction and the spread of protectionism can hurt her as much or more than most countries. Internally her economy faces problems arising from the high cost of land and agricultural products prices, high distribution costs, falling consumer demand attendant on low population growth and an ageing population, unemployment and excessive government borrowing because of enormous budget deficits. In brief, Japan suffers as much as other countries when world trade diminishes.

Nevertheless, Japan has joined the front rank of the world's advanced nations. As the West has not yet formulated a world-embracing strategy, or set an example in this direction, there is an opportunity for Japan to emerge as a leader. She could become a model for developing nations, but to do so she must know her own experiences and be able to explain them. To be a source of culture she must evaluate her traditional traits and see for herself their strengths and weaknesses. She must, somehow, break down the barriers her system erects between insiders and outsiders, both domestically and internationally. She must gain self-confidence to act in genuine co-operation with other nations. Her example could be an inspiration for both advanced and developing countries throughout the world.

If we agree that Japan is an advanced industrial and commercial country, and who can deny it, should we not concede that Japan's competitive-communism is an advanced social system?

Bibliography

BURUMA, IAN, *A Japanese Mirror* (London: Jonathan Cape, 1984).

CLARK, GREGORY, *Nihonjin-Yuniikusa no Gensen* (Tokyo: Simul Press, 1977).

DOI, TAKEO *The Anatomy of Dependence* (Tokyo: Kodansha International, 1973).

——, *The Anatomy of Self* (Tokyo: Kodansha International, 1986).

HASEGAWA, NYOZEKAN, *Japanese National Character* (Tokyo: Board of Tourist Industry, 1942).

HANAMI, TADASHI, *Labor Relations in Japan Today* (Tokyo: Kodansha International, 1979).

IMAI, MASAAKI, *Never Take Yes for an Answer* (Tokyo: Simul Press, 1975).

——, *16 Ways to Avoid Saying No* (Tokyo: Nihon Keizai Shinbun, 1981).

——, *Kaizen, the Key to Japan's Competitive Success*, (New York: Random House, 1986).

LEBRA, TAKIE SUGIYAMA, *Japanese Patterns of Behavior* (Honolulu: University Press of Hawaii, 1976).

LEE, O-YOUNG, *Small is Better* (Tokyo: Kodansha International, 1984).

MILLER, ROY ANDREW, *The Japanese Language in Contemporary Japan* (Washington, D.C.: American Enterprise Institute for Public Policy Research, 1977).

McCORMACK, GAVIN; SUGIMOTO, YOSHIO, *Democracy in Contemporary Japan* (New York: M. E. Sharpe Inc., 1986).

MOORE, CHARLES A., *The Japanese Mind* (Tokyo: Charles E. Tuttle Company, 1973).

REISCHAUER, EDWIN O., *The Japanese* (Tokyo: Charles E. Tuttle Company, 1978).

STEVEN, ROB, *Classes in Contemporary Japan* (Cambridge University Press, 1984).

TSUNODA, TADANOBU, *Nihonjin no No* (The Japanese Brain) (Tokyo: Taishukan, 1978).

Index

Other Tuttle Titles of Interest

THE JAPANESE TODAY: CHANGE AND CONTINUITY *by Edwin O. Reischauer*

"Edwin Reischauer displays a novelist's sensitivity in this thorough overview, managing to explain the paradoxes of Japan without diminishing the sense of mystery."

—*The Los Angeles Times*

SCIENCE & CULTURE IN TRADITIONAL JAPAN *by Masayoshi Sugimoto and David L. Swain*

"Among the numerous books on Japan and Japanese history, this one is unique in presenting an adequate survey of the history of science and learning in Japan for the first time in a Western language."

—Masao Watanabe
The American Scientist

SECOND TO NONE: AMERICAN COMPANIES IN JAPAN *by Robert C. Christopher*

"A timely, highly readable book."

—*New York Times*

"Rare is the European or American who understands Japan as well as this author."

—*Nihon Keizai Shimbun*

SETTING UP & OPERATING A BUSINESS IN JAPAN: A HANDBOOK FOR THE FOREIGN BUSINESSMAN *by Helene Thian*

> "A unique handbook, speaking to the key issues and drawing on the experiences of veterans at the Japan business game."
>
> —James C. Abegglen

MITI AND THE JAPANESE MIRACLE: THE GROWTH OF INDUSTRIAL POLICY, 1925–1975 *by Chalmers Johnson*

> "Johnson sets out to explain and in the process to demystify the reasons for Japanese economic success by concentrating on the one institution which perhaps more than any other has been responsible for achieving that success: the Ministry of International Trade and Industry (MITI). It is a daunting task admirably undertaken by Johnson . . . who has produced a rich, suggestive, and stimulating book."
>
> —*Far Eastern Economic Review*

THE JAPANESE MIND: THE GOLIATH EXPLAINED *by Robert C. Christopher*

> "A very perceptive, well-informed, interesting and also amusing look at contemporary Japan and its position in the world."
>
> —Edwin O. Reischauer

> "Christopher's significant book drives home a centrally important message: not technique but culture is the key to Japan's success."
>
> —Zbigniew Brzezinski

JAPAN: THE FRAGILE SUPERPOWER (2nd revised edition) *by Frank Gibney*

> "One of the best panoramic views of Japan to have been published within memory."
>
> —*The New Republic*

> "One of the finest books written on Asia by any American . . . readable, enjoyable, exciting, powerful, important, a book written to last."
>
> —Theodore H. White

HOW TO DO BUSINESS WITH THE JAPANESE: A STRATEGY FOR SUCCESS *by Mark Zimmerman*

> "Precisely what an able Western businessman coming to Japan wants to know, by an astute, hard-working business leader who got the nuances right."
>
> —Ezra F. Vogel

THE JAPANESE COMPANY *by Rodney Clark*

> "Mr. Clark has written an excellent analysis [of the Japanese company] that should stand the tests of time and competition to become a definitive work in the genre."
>
> —*Wall Street Journal*

KAISHA: THE JAPANESE CORPORATION *by James C. Abegglen and George Stalk, Jr.*

> "If I were a U.S. manager trying to understand the anatomy of a Japanese racer breathing hard at my shoulder, I'd read this book."
>
> —*Wall Street Journal*